ADVICE MATTERS

TONY JEARY
JAY D. RODGERS

Clovercroft Publishing

Advice Matters

©2015 by Tony Jeary and Jay D. Rodgers

Published by Clovercroft Publishing, Franklin, Tennessee.

Published in association with Larry Carpenter of Christian Book Services, LLC.
www.christianbookservices.com

Support Writing by Nonie Jobe

Cover Design by Eddie Renz

Interior Design by Adept Content Solutions

Printed in the United States of America

978-1-972557-31-0

CONTENTS

INTRODUCTION

"A wise person learns from both the successes and mistakes of others." While this quote, in one form or another, may not be original to us, it defines a life principle that has shaped our lives and careers probably as much as any other. It's precisely because we have witnessed firsthand the power of this principle over the years, and because we believe so strongly in the truth it conveys, that we are writing this book.

> **"IF WE NEVER RECEIVED ANY FRESH, NEW IDEAS FROM OTHERS, OUR ONLY OPTIONS WOULD BE TO KEEP DOING THE SAME THINGS THE SAME WAY WE HAVE ALWAYS DONE THEM —AND KEEP GETTING BASICALLY THE SAME RESULTS."**
> **—TONY JEARY**

The utter strength of this truth inspired Tony to devote a chapter to it in a book he wrote a few years ago called *Success Acceleration*. Here's a quote from that chapter: "If we never received any fresh, new ideas from others, our only options would be to keep doing the same things the same way we have always done them – and keep getting basically the same results." It's simple, really; if we want different results, we need new thinking. New information stimulates both our reasoning processes and our creative juices and helps us think better. We can get this information from one of two sources— observations from our own experiences, which is definitely helpful, or from other people. If our progress is limited, though, to our own observations, we could be in for a long, slow process. Learning strategically from the wisdom and insight of others helps us to be more successful *faster*. Remember, in today's market speed often is our competitive advantage and directly impacts our ability to compete and win.

In the words of 17th century poet John Donne, "No man is an island." Most highly successful people will tell you that they could not have even begun their journey without the encouragement, support, and advice of the people around them. We have both been extremely successful in our careers, and we credit much of our success to the advice we have received from others. What an incredible privilege to be able to turn around and give back what we have received in such abundance.

For years, both Tony and Jay have poured advice and counsel into the lives of others. Tony has personally advised and coached the presidents of Ford, TGI Fridays, Sam's Club, New York Life, Wal-Mart, Firestone, Samsung, and Qualcomm, as well as countless other top leaders and achievers. Jay has been a successful entrepreneur who personally founded, grew, and sold over a dozen businesses, involving millions of net profit dollars. He has had tremendous success in his entrepreneurial projects and is past the age when most people want to kick back and retire. Yet, instead of slowing down at this stage of his life, he decided to throw his energy into founding and operating Biz Owners Ed, Inc., a 501(c)(3) non-profit, for the sole purpose of mentoring serious entrepreneurs and helping them succeed (http://bizownersed.org/). Together, Tony and Jay have helped thousands of open-minded high achievers reach levels of success that very few attain.

You're never too young or too old to benefit from great advice from others – or to give it away – and you can never reach a level of success where you no longer need it. When Tony was 17 years old and still a senior in high school, he started seeking advice from many of his parents' friends so he could learn business, and that's what launched his early success. He and Jay have a mutual friend, Peter Thomas, who has been a serial entrepreneur for more than four decades, specializing in franchising and real estate. Peter has developed billions of dollars in real estate projects, including shopping centers, apartments, condominiums, and golf courses, and he built Century 21 all across Canada. The second time Tony met him, Peter arranged for them to meet on his yacht. With all of his successes, within one hour of that meeting, he said to Tony, "I want you to be my coach for life."

Jay has been Tony's business mentor for years. Yet, because he believes so strongly in the impact that great advice can have, he recently took the management team of a company he founded to Tony's studio for a strategic planning session and asked Tony to "Pour it on!" The results have been no less than amazing. In the past 90 days, the company has enjoyed more profit growth than they experienced in the prior twelve months. More importantly, they have now focused on a niche market that they are uniquely qualified to serve.

Because of their track records and the fact that their lives and careers have been so immersed in the giving and receiving of advice, they both speak from a unique perspective that should give you, the reader, total confidence that what they say has been lived out for decades. This book is not theory; it's built on the experiences of two top advisors who have both made (and lost) millions, who have both built successful lives, and who have both exponentially benefited from the advice of others. Their lives have played out the powerful truth that "advice matters."

Jay and Tony were connected by a mutual colleague, Robert Fielder. As his client,

JAY'S ELABORATE LIGHT FIXTURE, WHICH DOUBLES AS A CONFERENCE TABLE, HAS ETCHED IN ITS GLASS TOP THE LOGOS OF OVER 20 COMPANIES HE HAS BUILT AND SOLD. TONY WAS IMPRESSED WITH SUCH LEVEL OF DETAIL FROM THE FIRST DAY HE MET JAY AND CONTINUES TO BE IMPRESSED AS THEIR MENTORSHIP AND FRIENDSHIP GROW. JAY IS A MAN OF MUCH WISDOM, AND HE MODELS SHARING IT EFFECTIVELY WITH OTHERS WHO ARE COMMITTED TO ENTREPRENEURIAL SUCCESS.

Robert was in Tony's studio one day, and he said, "There's a guy you have to meet! He's a partner of mine in a business venture, and he's just like you!" Jay happened to live near Tony, although they had never met. Tony did some research and discovered that Jay was, indeed, a person he wanted to meet; so he called and scheduled an appointment with him. When Tony went to Jay's office, which is built to look like a barn, Jay pushed a button on the wall, and the elaborate light fixture came down from the ceiling and became a conference table! He pointed out that the conference table had 20 or so logos etched on it of companies that he had either started or played a major role in growing. Jay said, "Let's get to work"; they sat down with their legal pads, each with his own list of about six to eight things he wanted to discuss, and the rest is history. Because they were both open-minded, they were able to create a healthy mentoring relationship that has lasted for years. Within weeks of meeting, they flew from Dallas to New York for a day just to have lunch with one of Jay's colleagues who could give Tony advice that would help him with a new client (which would prove to be the first of many mutually profitable introductions).

In the years since then, Jay has mentored Tony – usually monthly – and they have become trusted colleagues, friends, and now co-authors. Their desire is to give back to the world a small portion of what they have been given as the recipients of great advice from others, and to create a book that would hopefully be impactful for those open-minded people who really want to do life and business better.

SECTION I:
WHY GET ADVICE?

CHAPTER 1

LISTENING IS THE PATH TO THINKING—HENCE BETTER CHOICES, BETTER DECISIONS, AND BETTER RESULTS

"The mind is not a vessel that needs filling,
but wood that needs igniting."
—PLUTARCH

Alan Dreeben had grown his company from a small South Texas distributor to a multi-state organization, with revenue of about $2 billion and over 2,000 associates. It was 2001, and he was in New York City having lunch with Claude Giroux and Jay, classmates from the Harvard Owners/ Presidents Management Program they had attended together some eleven years before. Claude was a citizen of the world and a unique individual. As they walked to the restaurant, Alan told Claude that he was thinking of leaving his company – the company he had grown from one location to a national corporation. Additional management had been brought in as part of a merger, and he wasn't sure that his voice was still being heard by the executive team in the midst of the growth and expansion. He didn't want to stay there if he didn't have significant input throughout the organization. Claude looked at him with disbelief and said, "That's the dumbest thing I've ever heard. There's such a simple answer to your issue."

"If it's so easy, what is it?" Alan asked.

"In a merger, the way to prevail," Claude explained, "is to be sure you are the head of the compensation committee."

"We don't have a compensation committee," Alan answered.

"Then form one," Claude retorted. "All large companies need one. And make yourself the chairman!"

So that's exactly what Alan did; and to this day, he has the attention of all of the top executives. They discuss with him what they are doing, what their objectives are, and what their challenges and successes are. The company has since grown to over 9,000 associates with a revenue of over $6 billion. With that one bit of wisdom and strategic thinking, Claude provided the perfect advice for Alan's critical business challenge.

Advice matters. No matter what your age, outstanding advice can propel your company, your career, and your life forward, just like it did for Alan Dreeben. Alan was in his 50s at the time; and he made the best career decision in his life when he listened to and acted on Claude's advice. Claude, who was in his late 60s, had made a lot of wise decisions throughout his career and had the successes to prove it. He had just sold his worldwide company, which he had started on a shoestring, for well over $100 million in cash. Seeking remarkable advice over the years from Claude and others has enabled Alan to lead his company to the outstanding success it enjoys today.

IF YOU WANT EXTRAORDINARY RESULTS, SEEK ADVICE FROM PEOPLE WHO HAVE PRODUCED EXTRAORDINARY RESULTS.

Seeking advice from others who have achieved the kind of results you're looking for is one of the wisest – and quickest – ways to design and live a successful life, grow your business, and hit that next level of success you've been endeavoring to reach. In fact, seeking advice is often the crucial piece of the success puzzle that catapults your results into an arena you could never have achieved alone.

Learning from the experiences of others, both their mistakes and their successes, helps you think better and thus leads to making better decisions, a better business, and a better life. Wise advice can also help you avoid pitfalls that could derail your success. If you want extraordinary results, seek advice from people who have produced extraordinary results. Jay likes to say it this way: "If you want to be moderately successful, choose a moderately successful advisor. If you aspire to be insanely successful, choose an advisor who has been insanely successful."

THE *BELIEF WINDOW*

We all conduct our lives and make decisions based on the principles that are on our *Belief Window*. We filter life and process information through those principles, which we began forming from birth from things our parents and teachers taught us, our own experiences, and our observations of the world around us. Since we filter our thoughts and actions through the principles on our *Belief Window*, it affects everything we see, hear, and experience. We form our "life rules," and then establish a behavior pattern according to those rules. If we're not constantly re-evaluating and updating the principles on our *Belief Window* as the world changes and the rules evolve, they can become obsolete and ineffective in our decision making.

As we go through life, we are constantly making value judgments, forming opinions, interpreting events, and making decisions about the things we will and will not do. Our *Belief Window* functions as a filtering device for all this. If our principles are accurate, they help us make right choices. If our *Belief Window* contains inaccurate principles, though, there will be significant errors in the way information is filtered, and our ideas and choices will be impacted.

> **"THE TEAM WITH THE BEST PLAYERS WINS."**
> **— JACK WELCH**

For example, you may have been brought up to believe, like many of us, that you should always clean up your plate when you're eating a meal. By now, you may realize that this is an inaccurate (and unhealthy) principle you adopted on your *Belief Window* from the past, and you probably understand the importance of managing portion control. You know that you should move your plate away when you start getting full, so you won't overeat. Some people had that inaccurate principle so entrenched on their *Belief Window*, though, that they still feel guilty today when they don't clean their plate, instead of feeling good that they had the discipline to move it away and not overeat.

You may have also been taught to believe that "Sticks and stones may break our bones, but words will never harm us." Maybe you don't think you had ever accepted that as a true principle on your *Belief Window*. Think about this, though: What you say to people, or even what you call them, can impact their lives a lot longer than a black eye. What you say to an employee or your child, for example, can sometimes impact who that person becomes. And what someone like an advisor says to you can give you confidence and make a substantial difference in how you see yourself. So that may be an inaccurate principle you need to correct in your *Belief Window* to remind you to keep your own words positive and encouraging.

Since everything we do is based on the principles on our *Belief Window*, we have to constantly ensure that the principles we believe to be true are, in fact, true and up to date. We do this by studying, by intentional personal and group reflection, and by seeking outstanding advice and counsel. The right advisors will help us make the right choices based on accurate and current information.

A few years ago, Tony realized that he carried a flawed principle on his *Belief Window*. He believed that the best way to stay abreast of everything when he traveled was to have his staff fax to him at his hotel each night all of his important mail and any information he needed to make decisions. One day a trusted colleague suggested that email would be more efficient than faxing. He said, "No, we have perfected this system over the years, and it's what works best for me." As he reflected on it later, though, he realized that his colleague was right; that principle on his *Belief Window* was outdated. He adjusted it and changed his system over to email, and that simple modification has made a world of positive difference in the way he communicates with his staff.

Here's another example: In Jay's early education, training, and career, he was taught to believe that an entrepreneur should set up his business as a Sub S corporation, rather than a C Corp, in order to avoid double taxation on exit if the buyer insisted on buying assets (rather than stock), as most buyers do. Today, the best answer for an entrepreneur in most cases is an LLC or an LP. Technology is constantly changing, and so is the Internal Revenue Code; and we often have to make adjustments in our *Belief Window* in order to keep up with those changes.

Getting wise advice helps you constantly refine your *Belief Window* with accurate truisms, principles, rules, and ways of thinking. As you make adjustments on your *Belief Window* based on that advice, you correct erroneous beliefs and create more accurate thinking.

Everyone wants to win. Remember, as you travel the road to success, that for every mile of road, there are two miles of ditch. There are many things that can cause you to get off into the ditch, on one side or the other, even though you may have years of success behind you. You need to constantly adjust and correct your course to make sure you stay out of the ditches. The best way to ensure that you stay in the middle of the lane is to constantly have advisors by your side to help keep your *Belief Window* unpolluted.

How does that work? Sometimes your advisors will give you information that adjusts your *Belief Window* during the course of a conversation. It could come in the form of a correction of something you have believed true for years, or it could be something new that causes an "ah-ha" moment. Or one of your advisors may send you a really great quote from a book or a very successful person, and you realize it's a general guiding principle that you need to put into your *Belief Window* and own for life. It may even be a truism that has played out well in your advisor's life or business, and you realize you would do well to incorporate it onto your *Belief Window*. For example, your mentor may help you with the best wording for a certain clause in a contract; and from that, you may get a truism that goes something like this: "Always consider the other party's positions and desires when you are suggesting a change to the contract."

Jay benefited tremendously from two such clauses drafted by his long-time advisor, David Hammer. One was a small clause in the contract for the purchase of his condo. Jay was reluctant to buy the condo because the real estate market was very strong and he feared a downturn in the market would reduce the value of the condo. After the seller assured Jay that he would never lower the prices, David added a clause to the contract that nailed down that assurance, which ultimately resulted in a $172,500 rebate when the residential market cooled and the seller did lower his prices.

In the other case, Jay was selling one of his companies for a combination of cash and stock. The stock, though, was restricted and would not be sellable for several months. If the stock were to drop in value during that time, it would, in essence, reduce the sales price for Jay's company. David put a small clause into the definitive agreement that protected the value of the stock, which yielded several hundred thousand dollars in additional cash when the price of the stock dropped.

David's crafting of these two clauses generated a new (and profitable) truism in Jay's *Belief Window*: Always look for creative ways to protect and/or ensure the outcome you desire.

You may think that "getting advice" is about finding someone to help you make a decision. "Do I sell or not sell?" "Do I go this way or that way?" Yes, it can be about seeking advice to help you make specific decisions. In the bigger picture, though, it's about getting the *right principles* on your *Belief Window;* so as you're doing life – including business – you're able to grab advice from the people around you and make decisions on an ongoing basis that significantly impact your results. When you seek out counsel from your advisors, constantly be on the lookout for ways to sharpen what's on your *Belief Window*, whether it's through a principle, a truism, a quote, or a specific piece of advice. Your goal should be to have the highest level of accuracy in your *Belief Window* so you can make the best decisions possible.

We will get more into choosing the right advisors in Chapters 2 and 3, but we want to issue a word of caution here: Before you get locked into a particular advisor – particularly a paid professional advisor like a CPA – one thing to consider is that advisor's schedule. Sometimes advisors these days are a lot like mechanics; they have a process that they have to go through, whether it's filling out a tax return or preparing a definitive agreement; and they've done it so many times that they don't always think about what it means every time they do it. And thinking about what it means *to you* can ultimately lead to the key piece of advice they can provide to help you re-evaluate and update your *Belief Window*. Be sure you get an advisor who is in the moment and cares about your particular situation so he or she can help you maintain an accurate *Belief Window*.

LOGIC AND INTUITION

Good decision-making should be a combination of logic and intuition. Sometimes we use more logic, which is based on reasoning; and sometimes we use more intuition, which we often call our "gut feeling." Neither is better than the other; they just have different advantages and applications. Often the best decisions are made when we use a good mix of both.

Generally speaking, when you're getting advice, you're getting logic. Your advisor may say something like, "Let me give you my thinking on this," and you add that advice to the logic side of the equation, along with your own reasoning. Then you need to be able to add your intuition to that and make a good, solid decision. Sometimes you may want to ask your advisor for both his or her intuition and logic.

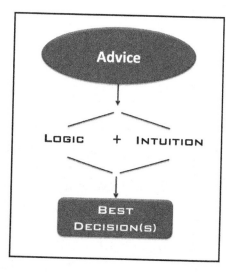

In all the companies he has owned throughout his business career, Jay has insisted that every applicant for every position be interviewed by three people - the three that are the most directly involved with that particular new hire. And because he understood the importance of using both logic and intuition in any hiring decision, any one of those three people were allowed to blackball the interviewee without giving a reason for it, which allowed intuition to play a role in the decision. If the person had been required to give a reason, it would have negated the role of intuition and thrown the decision back into the realm of logic.

THE FOUR LEVELS OF ADVICE AND RESULTS

One of the most important things to remember in getting advice is that the results you get from that advice will be a direct reflection of the credentials and expertise of the source. If you get good advice, you'll get good results; and if you get great advice, you'll get great results. What you really want, though, is Mastery advice, because the transition from great to Mastery has a colossal impact on your results. It goes back to our statement that if you want outstanding results, you need to get advice from people that produce outstanding results. Mastery advice comes from someone who's been down the road you want to travel, experienced it, created it, lived it, and has a track record of exceptional results.

There's a fourth level of advice, though, that you need to watch out for and avoid at all costs – and that's bad advice. Getting bad advice can be just as detrimental as (or worse than) getting no advice at all. Two prominent examples come to mind: Ford Motor Company's fiasco with the Edsel and Coca Cola's disaster with New Coke. In both cases, the companies designed a product for which there was no market. They failed to remember that you cannot *create* a market; you can only *serve* one. The advice they moved forward on was bad advice.

ONE OF THE MOST IMPORTANT THINGS TO REMEMBER IN GETTING ADVICE IS THAT THE RESULTS YOU GET FROM THAT ADVICE WILL BE A DIRECT REFLECTION OF THE CREDENTIALS AND EXPERTISE OF THE SOURCE.

Tony has a model that he demonstrates through a visual called the *Mastery Impact Curve*. This model gives a visual representation of a person's level of effectiveness in any particular area, and it illustrates the exponential difference in results when that individual moves from bad to good to great, and then to Mastery. Notice in the *Mastery Impact Curve* model below that the impact increases most significantly when effectiveness is achieved in the Mastery level. You can see that seeking advice on the first two levels can potentially produce minimal results, and the curve rises noticeably when you seek great advice; yet the curve rises dramatically when you seek advice from the Masters, which yields extraordinary results.

Here's an example: Jay once had two CPAs working for him. As it happened, both men were at his offices on the same day. One stayed in the office at one end of the hall, recording history and counting beans; the other spent his time in Jay's office analyzing the financial statements and using that information to make projections and suggestions for their operation the next year and the year after. One gave minimal (good) advice; the other, because of his own history and track record as an entrepreneur, gave Mastery advice. Which one do you think helped take the company's results over the top?

In another incident, Jerry, a longtime friend, called Jay and said, "I have received an offer for my company. I'm ready to retire, and it's time to sell. Would you advise me?" Jay agreed and arranged for his deal attorney, David Hammer, to be present at the meeting. It became immediately apparent that there was a challenge. Jerry had received bad advice from his attorney and/or CPA, and the company had been set up as a C Corp, rather than an S Corp. There had been at least a 20-year window when the company could have been converted to an S Corp with no adverse tax consequences. For all of those years, his advisors had simply

> **Mastery advice comes from someone who's been down the road you want to travel, experienced it, created it, lived it, and has a track record of exceptional results.**

been checking the boxes and filling out the forms. They had never gotten involved enough to give Jerry the Master advice he actually needed.

As is typically the case, the buyer's offer was to buy the assets of the company, not the stock. Buyers normally refuse to buy stock because of the liabilities associated with the stock purchase. Selling all the assets of his C Corp would have meant that Jerry would have had to pay over 50 percent of the proceeds from the sale in taxes. Jerry had to turn the offer down and walk away. The conversion to the S Corp has now been made. Unfortunately, Jerry will have to postpone his retirement and continue running the business for at least five more years until all of the tax consequences of the conversion are removed.

SEEK INPUT FROM PEOPLE WITH THE RIGHT HISTORY AND EXPERTISE WHO WILL SHINE A LIGHT ON OPTIONS AND COURSES OF ACTION YOU MAY NOT HAVE THOUGHT OF OR THE POSSIBLE CONSEQUENCES OF THE VARIOUS CHOICES THAT ARE BEFORE YOU.

There are some non-profit organizations out there providing mentors to give free advice to small businesses. You might go to one and get a great advisor – but there's also a good chance that you could get someone who just wants to get out of the house after retirement. Be forewarned that excellence is often not one of the criteria these sources require of advisors. These are people who may or may not have experienced success; and if they had, was it passable, acceptable, or incredible success? If you sign up to get advice from these organizations just because of the budget you would save, and you pick someone you know nothing about as far as his or her background, experience, or successes, you could really end up running down a trail that could be disastrous. Your best bet is to extensively research the advisor you are considering before you get into a relationship. Find out how successful his or her career is or was. The more you verify that your advisor has an outstanding track record, the better your chances are for getting Mastery advice and Mastery results.

On the flip side of that, when Tony is approached by prospective clients who want to hire him as their coach or strategist, or when Jay is asked to mentor someone, they both research the individuals extensively before agreeing to advise them. They've both done things for decades that have positioned them as Master advisors (and we'll get into that more in Chapter 3, Gathering Your Advisors), so a lot of people seek them out. They both enjoy the win; so they only accept clients/mentees who are committed to winning, knowing that their advice can make a major impact on the speed and magnitude of their win. They have helped people and corporations make millions upon millions of dollars. People often ask them, "How do you always win?" Part of the answer to that question is that they pick winners – people who are more committed to

> "I THINK THE GREATEST THING WE GIVE EACH OTHER IS ENCOURAGEMENT... KNOWING THAT I'M TALKING TO SOMEONE IN THIS MENTORING RELATIONSHIP WHO'S INTERESTED IN THE BIG IDEA HERE IS VERY, VERY IMPORTANT TO ME. I THINK IF IT WERE JUST ABOUT HELPING ME GET TO THE NEXT STEP, IT WOULD BE A HECK OF A LOT LESS INTERESTING."
> —ANNE SWEENEY, PRESIDENT OF DISNEY/ABC TELEVISION GROUP

winning, who take action, and who already have a track record of success. And they are both in a position to do that because they themselves have had such great counsel from Master advisors for decades.

It's very important that you understand the true purpose of having advisors: To seek input from people with the right history and expertise who will shine a light on options and courses of action you may not have thought of or the possible consequences of the various choices that are before you. It is *not* to find people who will make decisions for you. You must always remember that it's your time, your money, your business, your life, your risk – and your final decision.

Be particularly vigilant when seeking advice from CPAs and attorneys, and consider their advice within the scope of their expertise and history. In most cases, they should not suggest a single specific solution or a specific course of action for you. Unless the attorney or CPA happens to have unusual qualifications as an entrepreneur or business executive, his or her job is to evaluate and point out to you the risks and ramifications involved in the various choices available to you. Keep in mind, also, that attorneys and CPAs typically have a risk tolerance that is totally different from yours. Don't fall into the trap of letting them make business decisions for you. They are advisors, who are to give you the facts and analyses, along with the accompanying details, that help you make the best decisions. You, as the entrepreneur or corporate executive, should study and evaluate the advice that was given, and then always make the final decisions yourself.

> **THE MORE YOU VERIFY THAT YOUR ADVISOR HAS AN OUTSTANDING TRACK RECORD, THE BETTER YOUR CHANCES ARE FOR GETTING MASTERY ADVICE AND MASTERY RESULTS.**

Having said that, Jay and Tony both have extraordinary advisors who are the classic exceptions to that rule. David Hammer, who is both an attorney and a CPA, has served as Jay's special business colleague, advisor, and attorney, supporting his business decisions for almost three decades. David joined the entrepreneurial world about fifteen years ago by opening his own investment banking firm to facilitate mergers and acquisitions in the 10-to-100 million-dollar range. That ongoing longevity and refinement of successes has put him in a very strong position to both participate in deals and give advice, and he is a very impactful entrepreneur in his own right.

David was referred by a man who served on a bank board with Jay when he was looking for a lawyer to handle the sale of one of his companies (which he ended up selling to a New York Stock Exchange firm for $4.5 million, debt free, back in the 80s when that was a lot of money).

Jay was about two years out from selling the company, and finding the right mergers and acquisitions lawyer was on his checklist. He took David to lunch, but at that time David had not learned to sell himself and his talents. Thinking he was not the right man, Jay marked him off the candidate list. About ten days later Jay was forming a corporation, a printing company, and the three principal players who were going to run it were coming up from Houston to meet with him on a Saturday. They needed to structure, set up, and prepare to register their entity that day. Jay called all the attorneys he knew, and they were all too busy playing golf to come out to his office on a Saturday. He remembered having had lunch with David, and thought, "Well, anybody could set up a Sub S corporation." He called, and David agreed to come out. Within five minutes they were finishing each other's sentences, and Jay knew it was a fit. Since then David has become an exemplary Master advisor and has closed the sale of 13 of Jay's companies.

Frank Adams is another notable exception. When Jay was selling Healthcare Staff Resources, Inc. (HSR), the company he initially interviewed David to handle (which he later did), a prospective buyer came out and brought Frank, his CPA, with him. Jay was so impressed with Frank that he told him, "If your client buys this company, you can do the closing numbers for both of us. It'll be faster and more efficient." Later, he brought Frank in to be the CEO of another company, Physician Staffing Resources, Inc. (PSR), with the assignment of selling the company. That was 18 years ago. Frank and his partner David Singley acquired equity and stayed with the acquiring company; and when the PSR division was sold again last year, they each collected a $5 million check and were given significant stock in the buyer's company. (By the way, Frank was the CPA we mentioned earlier who had given Jay Mastery advice, compared to the CPA who had given minimal advice. Frank's advice was given that day, not just from a CPA's standpoint, but also from the standpoint of an entrepreneur in his own right.)

Exceptional advisors like David Hammer and Frank Adams are definitely in the Mastery category. (Jay introduced David to Tony years ago, and David is now on Tony's life team as his deal attorney; Tony does not do deals without David's advice.)

V.I.P.s

- Seeking advice from others who have achieved the kind of results you're looking for is one of the wisest – and quickest – ways to design and live a successful life, grow your business, or hit that next level of success you've been endeavoring to reach.

- If you want extraordinary results, you need to seek advice from people who have produced extraordinary results.

- We all hold principles and philosophies on our *Belief Window* that filter not only how we view the world, but also the actions we take or don't take as we navigate through life. Since everything we do is based on the principles on our *Belief Window*, we have to constantly ensure that the principles we believe to be true are, in fact, true and up to date. We do this by studying, by intentional personal and group reflection, and by seeking outstanding advice and counsel.

- One of the most important things to remember in getting advice is that the results you get from that advice will be a direct reflection of the credentials and expertise of the source. Good advice will get you good results, and great advice will get you great results. The transition from great to Mastery, though, has a colossal impact on your results.

- There's a fourth level of advice that you need to watch out for and avoid at all costs – and that's bad advice.

- Unless advisors like attorneys or CPAs happen to have unusual qualifications as an entrepreneur, their job is to evaluate and point out to you the risks and ramifications involved in the various choices that lay in front of you. You, as the entrepreneur, should study and evaluate the advice that was given, and then always make the final decisions yourself.

SECTION II:
HOW TO GET ADVICE

CHAPTER 2:

START WITH THE WHERE: DEFINING YOUR OPTIONS

"Learning is truly a value, growth for every employee is a real objective, mistakes aren't always fatal, and there are lots of people around whom you can reach out to for coaching and mentoring."
—JACK WELCH, *WINNING*

About ten years ago, a coach and great friend Tony had had for years, the late Jim Norman, said to him, "Tony, up to this point most of your books have focused on presentation strategy. What you really do best, though, is help high achievers find strategic clarity." He said, "Why don't you write a new foundational best seller and present the concepts that have made such a powerful impact on your clients – clarity, focus, and execution?" Tony knew instantly that it was the perfect effort to really leverage his expertise.

He carefully wrote up his methodology and validated it with a few clients, including the U.S. Senate in a training session for its managers in Washington, D.C. The response was phenomenal. They were off and running.

Tony had authored over three dozen books up to that point, so by that time he had developed many relationships with NYC publishers as well as agents. He gathered advice from some of his contacts about the new book and decided on a title, *Strategic Acceleration: Succeed at the Speed of Life.* Then Tony, Jim (his coach) and his literary agent met with Perseus in New York. Perseus decided to publish the book under its brand Vanguard Press. With its launch in 2009, Tony's entire professional focus shifted to helping his clients really achieve what he calls *Strategic Clarity*.

That advice that Tony received from his coach resulted in a monumental turning point in his career. It catapulted him into an arena where he could give even more value to his clients. Hundreds of successful top executives and entrepreneurs began reaching out to engage him and his team to bring clarity, focus, and execution to their world. In the six years since publishing *Strategic Acceleration*, Tony's new moniker has become The RESULTS Guy™.

The most successful people understand that they need to surround themselves with individuals who can pour into them the wisdom and knowledge they need to excel. Your chances of success increase exponentially when you seek the advice of others who are already extremely successful and are willing to invest in your life by sharing their experiences and learned success principles. If you already have a mentor and/or a coach with whom you meet on a regular schedule to help you take your life and business to the next level, we would guess that you are probably ahead of about 98 percent of the business people in the world. We believe that those who are trying to attain success with no professional coach or mentor relationship are severely handicapping themselves in their pursuit of extreme success.

When most people consider seeking advice to help them make wise decisions and improve their results, they primarily think of coaches and mentors. We believe there are actually six sources of advice available:

1. Coaches
2. Mentors
3. Trusted colleagues (including family)
4. Paid professional advisors (attorneys, CPAs, etc.)
5. Resources (like books, videos, and URLs)
6. Yourself (self-reflection)

A question we are asked often is, "What is the difference between a mentor and a coach?" Another goes something like this: "Can't my attorney or CPA provide all of the advice I need?" What we want to do for you in this chapter is to bring clarity to the roles each of these six sources play in giving advice.

COACHES AND MENTORS

While coaches and mentors both help you uncover *Blind Spots* and can significantly advance your life and career to the next level, there is a difference. Each has its own distinctive advantage and drawbacks. Understanding that money is a consideration when engaging a coach, ideally you will surround yourself with at least one coach and one or more mentors. Choose people who will challenge and inspire you to be your best and who will give you the benefit of their wisdom, experience, and insight.

A couple of years ago Tony wrote a book called *Living in the Black: My Blessed Life*, which was an autobiography of sorts in which he imparted 30 years of studying, living, and sharing distinctions of successful living. He related in the book some of the amazing benefits he has received from his coaches and mentors, and he explained the difference between the two:

> *I call coaching the "secret weapon of many of the world's top achievers." Few people automatically understand what it takes to reach their goals, overcome their weaknesses, and grow their strengths. One-on-one coaching can advance your career, grow your leadership skills, help you build your brand, and uncover Blind Spots. And with my Strategic Acceleration methodology, I also help my clients gain strategic clarity, develop focused plans, and execute more effectively. The right coach can take you to the next level, where you see a significant increase in your income, reach your goals faster, and become stronger in all areas of your life.*
>
> *When you connect with the right coach for you, it's an investment—not an expense—and it should pay short, medium, and long-term dividends. The right coach should dramatically alter the results of your life.*
>
> *Another great way to pinpoint the right things to do and stay on track is to seek the advice of one or two mentors who can help you see life better and get more of the results you want. A mentor is often a veteran in your field or has been somewhere you want to go—someone who has "been there, done that" and can keep you from falling into pitfalls that he or she may or may not have avoided. Ideally, a mentor is someone who is strong in the areas where you know you are weak. There are a lot of smart people around you, and you can excel and get better results by tapping into their advice. Identify one or two people who would be willing to take you on as a mentee, and take advantage of their wisdom, experience, and insight. Ask questions and seek their counsel. Mentors*

can often give you invaluable advice on personal and family mat-
ters, too, if you have the kind of relationship where you feel com-
fortable seeking their input.

Tony has been fortunate to have had his own two personal life coaches for decades – Mark Pantak has been his coach for half of his life, and Jim Norman was his coach for over 15 years, until we lost him recently to cancer. Tony believes that the power of having these two amazing men in his life – cheering him on, pulling for his success, sharing their wisdom, pointing out his key strengths, and constantly challenging him to find new perspective and different solutions to achieve his goals – has quantum-leaped his thinking, and hence his decision-making, and ultimately his success.

Tony also attributes his success to the excellent mentors he's had over the years (including Jay). They have poured into his life in so many ways: sharing how to shape his business deals and balance his investments, connecting him to great people, opening doors for him, encouraging him, reviewing his manuscripts, talking about what's next with his kids, and helping him to think and perform at a whole different level. Mentors do not charge for their advice; it's a way of giving back to help other people win and can be a source of major satisfaction when the mentor/mentee relationship is outstanding.

Kim Cloud, one of Jay's mentee's, shares the impact that mentoring has made on her life and career:

I thought I knew it all. On January 23, 2013, I was Kim Cloud, business owner. A day later, Kim Cloud, Business Owner, began to be transformed. This may sound crazy, yet I realized that what had set me apart from other small business owners in my community was my high level of confidence. Having no idea what a "mass exodus" was, I found out quickly as I experienced it head on that day, and my level of self-confidence was extinguished – for the time being!

A large corporate salon just down the street had done a very efficient job of recruiting my stylists and technicians. The recruiter (or "stealer," as I like to label her) did an incredible job of drafting 24 professionals who had been with Cloud 9 for over 15 years. In retrospect, I realize how naive it was to operate a business under the belief that no one would ever leave. The same level of self-confidence that brought me success was now sabotaging that same success. I never considered the possibility that someone would exit. Really, though, the people who chose to leave just created room for new professionals who desired success and a team environment.

Was I perfect? Evidently not! Did I learn tons from that day forward? Absolutely! From whom? Mentors! The definition of mentor is a wise and trusted counselor or teacher. I reached out to men and women who knew much more about business and recovery than I did, and I learned so much! I remember one of the first things Jay Rodgers asked me was "Kim, when should you fire someone?" His answer: "The first time you think about it."

How would this mentor's advice have changed things? What would have happened if I had gotten rid of the cancer, the negative, the pessimist in my business? Although I'll never know for sure, I do believe that if I had had this advice sooner, I could have saved much of my staff.

My mentors helped me go line-by-line through my P&L. We cut the extras and the ridiculous. What I learned from such brilliant, motivating professionals, I still carry with me today. I don't operate in fear, but I operate wiser and more prepared, building back my confidence and success daily.

Mentors are key."

Tony is a coach and Jay is a mentor. Tony's clients cover the gamut, from presidents and CEOs of the largest companies in the world to successful entrepreneurs. Jay, who mentors for the satisfaction of giving back, focuses on serious committed entrepreneurs. And yet they have a lot in common. Throughout their lives, they have both invested a great deal of time hanging out with smart people whom they have identified as highly successful – and many of them have been their seniors with at least a decade, and sometimes a generation, more experience under their belts. Jay, who is Tony's mentor, is a generation ahead of Tony; and he has poured oceans of wisdom and insight into Tony from his many years of being a highly successful entrepreneur and a business leader. Like any Master advisor, Jay has helped Tony sharpen his brand, his thinking, and many of his life efforts.

For example, Jay has guided Tony's move into more results compensation. He has advised him that many clients prefer to have selected advisors who "have skin in the game." Through his agency (Tony Jeary International), Tony now works more with selected successful clients, helping them grow in sales, profits, and value, and takes a part of his fee (what he calls a "success fee") based on the results he brings. Clients often prefer this arrangement, because it involves fairly low risk and ensures alignment.

Jay helped Tony develop his agreement along those lines with USA Truck, structuring his fee based on the results he would bring to the client. Tony teamed up with the president and started coaching the executive team of USA Truck in February 2013, when their stock (USAK) was at $4.69. Twenty-four months later, the stock was at $30.45. Everyone won big. USA Truck and its shareholders were happy because they got incredible results, and Tony and his team were able to reap the reward of their efforts.

Jay also recognizes and appreciates Tony's extraordinary coaching skills, and he has taken the management team of one of his companies to Tony for coaching. Tony wanted to give back to Jay for all of the invaluable time, effort, and advice he had poured into him; at the same time, he wanted Jay to experience firsthand the "magic" (as his clients call it) that Tony brings to the table. Jay and his team went in expecting outstanding results, and that's exactly what they got. "We left the session saying, 'Okay, Tony has pointed out that our CEO has various strengths but is wearing too many hats. We need a second person that is equally as strong to run marketing and sales,'" Jay said. "That became our focus. We used Culture Index to help us find the right person. We ended up hiring the most expensive employee we've ever hired and sold him 15 percent of the company, at a bargain price. It took a little while, but the results have been phenomenal."

"Having two people at the top has worked out very well for them," Tony said. "And I was able to show Jay that I could bring them powerful new thinking in only four hours, just as I promised, and really deliver value for them."

It could be very helpful to departmentalize your mentors for the different roles you play in life, both personally and professionally. In other words, choose those who have done successfully what you want to do in any area of your life. For example, Tony has mentors who have daughters that are ten years older than his daughters; and for decades he has gone to them for insight because they've raised exceptional kids. (We'll talk more about departmentalizing your advisors in the next chapter, Gathering Your Advisors.)

You may be very surprised how easy it is to enlist the advice of highly successful people in a mentor/mentee relationship. When Jay was starting Biz Owners Ed (see the Biz Owners Ed Story at the end of the book), he discovered that many of them are, in fact, ready and willing to give back. They understand that their success ensued from the gift of advice from others.

Jay tells a story about the genesis of Biz Owners Ed that validates the dramatic difference an advisor can make in the life of an organization.

Before Biz Owners Ed, Inc., held the first ten-week program that commenced in January 2013, the founders spent over a year in preparation. They identified and brought on board the mentors, guest speakers, and professional advisors and spent many long hours structuring and designing the way the program would run and be presented. Early on in the planning phase, they hired as an advisor Hall Martin from the Texas Entrepreneur Network in Austin, who had spent most of his career working with entrepreneurial groups. He drove in from Austin to attend the Biz planning sessions, and his advice was not inexpensive. Hall definitely added value. However, as the planning neared completion, Jay was beginning to question if his input had been worth the expense incurred to the fledgling non-profit.

Jay's question was irrefutably put to rest at the next meeting. It had always been the strategy that the program would consist of 10 four-hour sessions; and the plan was for the sessions to run for five consecutive weeks, on Tuesday and Thursday evening from 4 pm to 8 pm. Changes to that schedule had never been discussed at prior meetings. At that meeting, however, Hall stood up with a well prepared factual presentation about why the schedule was too intense – it would not only overload the class members, but it would also overload the entire Biz team. He felt that not stretching the program out could destroy the board's otherwise outstanding vision. He was extremely convincing and left the Biz team with no doubt that he was correct. They changed the schedule to present the program once a week over ten consecutive weeks, in four-hour sessions each Tuesday evening from 4 PM to 8 PM. With the first session in January 2013, it was immediately apparent to all involved that Hall's advice had not only been correct – it had been critical. The advice transformed the program from what might have been a disaster, or at best a mediocre endeavor, to an incredible success.

All of the Biz team that work so hard to help serious, committed entrepreneurs grow their companies are in complete agreement: that one piece of advice Hall Martin gave them was worth several times all the compensation that he received. His fee was, and remains, the best money the Biz team ever spent.

If you're just starting your climb to greatness, you may want to start with mentors, since they don't charge for their time, until you reach the point where the investment in a coach is more than justified by the results. We encourage you to add a coach to your advisory team as quickly as possible, though, because coaches can have such a dramatic effect on your success. Their entire focus and priority are helping you achieve exceptional results, and their fees are relevant to the expertise they can bring toward that end. As you grow your organization, the fee may be inconsequential to the amount of added revenue that can be produced with a coach's proficiency.

> **"A MENTOR IS SOMEONE WHO SEES MORE TALENT AND ABILITY WITHIN YOU, THAN YOU SEE IN YOURSELF, AND HELPS BRING IT OUT OF YOU."**
>
> **—BOB PROCTOR**

Tony's fee for coaching major corporations – where there are millions and sometimes billions of dollars at stake – becomes miniscule when it is related to the impact he has on the results. For example, Tony has earned a substantial fee over the last few years for coaching the executives at Walmart, a $480-billion company, because of the results he has helped them achieve. Walmart executives were delighted with the knowledge and expertise he was able to bring to them from his experience in helping turn Chrysler around in the early 90s – specifically, developing a planned, organized, and systematic training methodology for a giant company. Obviously, though, a startup company might not be able to justify a strategist with Tony's level of expertise and track record.

Here's another example of the incredible value a coach can bring. This story was told to Jay by one of his Biz Owners Ed graduates:

> In 2011 we engaged an experienced business coach to help us negotiate a new, business-changing customer/partner relationship. For us, it was potentially a very large deal that required much navigation into unknown territory. We asked our coach to work with us all the way through the process and guide us through the decisions.
>
> While we were sitting at the negotiation table with this potential new customer's CEO, hoping that we could work out a long-term, multi-year contract, we discovered that they were under some unusually vulnerable circumstances with respect to their operations. We also learned that all of their assets, which we thought they owned, were actually foreclosed upon by a previous creditor. This previous creditor wanted re-payment of his loan... and did not want to keep all of these assets. We realized that the real driver/decision maker was not the CEO, but the new owner of their assets!
>
> Immediately following the meeting, our coach pulled us aside and said "This is an amazing opportunity and you need to take it!" I really had no idea what he was referring to. I had basically left the meeting thinking we had no deal, because their operations were about to go bust and the owner of the assets was not going to commit to a long-term contract with us. Our coach saw this differently.
>
> He said this was a golden opportunity – an opportunity to sweep in and buy the assets of this company from the current own-

*er for pennies on the dollar of their market value. "Excuse me...
buy their assets?????" "Yes!" Our coach understood negotiation
and business. He knew much more than I.*

*In short, we ultimately purchased the assets directly from the
new owner and took over the operations of the entire client base
and staff. The actual acquisition process was painful, very scary,
and downright nail biting until it was all complete. But it was the
biggest and best decision we could have ever made, and we would
never have pursued that angle without the guidance of our coach.*

*Take advice from people smarter than you are, and it will
change your life!*

You may be wondering why, as a successful advisor and coach to such
high profile clients who have achieved an extraordinary level of success,
Tony would need to have coaches in his own life. It's because he does what
he believes and teaches. He believes in constantly aiming for sharper thinking, sharper decisions, and sharper results, just as the story above illustrates.
To achieve mastery, even coaches need coaches. You're never too successful to have coaches. Besides the president of Walmart, Tony has assisted,
coached, and advised the presidents and/or CEOs of Sam's Club, Firestone,
Ford, Samsung, New York Life, American Airlines, TGI Fridays, and many
of the world's other top companies; and he has had exceptional mentors and
coaches who have helped him reach higher levels of success in his own life.

TRUSTED COLLEAGUES (INCLUDING FAMILY)

As you go through life, you often find people you relate to and admire,
and you may bounce things off of each other. Those people are not really
coaches or mentors; they are colleagues that you trust and look up to for
advice.

Jay and Tony have both identified people in their lives who have demonstrated that they think far beyond the way most people think, and they are
willing to trade some of their advice for advice from these trusted colleagues. There is a great reciprocal principle in play. For example, Tony may
send an email to his trusted colleagues saying, "I'm attaching some book
cover options for a new book I'm writing. Can you give me your thoughts?"

And they will email him back with their opinions. Then one of them may send him an email soliciting his opinion on a marketing document he or she is working on, and Tony will review it and send an email back with his input. They both go to their trusted colleagues often, because they have proven to be an invaluable source of wisdom and insight in their lives.

Sometimes these trusted colleagues may be clients or co-workers, or they may be friends, and sometimes they're family. Tony and Jay both recognize their fathers as trusted colleagues who have given and modeled for them invaluable Master advice over the years. And both gratefully acknowledge that advice given by their fathers has had a huge impact on their success. (See their individual stories below.)

Regardless of how trusted colleagues have come into your life, you recognize that these are people you can admire and trust. You respect the way they see the world, what they've done, and the successes they've had. And, based upon that, you would be wise to trade some of your time and advice for some of theirs.

My Father Advised by Modeling
by Tony Jeary

My dad is a special man who modeled how to serve people. Wow! What great business and life advice he gave me, without even saying a word. That's the kind of man my dad is.

My dad also modeled two other very important pieces of advice for me:

1. Make lots of contacts

2. Do more than people expect.

So much of my life today is based on advice from my father.

1. Every day I look for ways to serve those I touch.

2. Every day I live by my personal and company motto, "Give Value, and Do More Than Is Expected," resulting in thousands of referrals and testimonials from all over the world.

3. My dad saved business cards – hundreds of them, bound by rubber bands in his desk. I started out that way. Today, of course, my contact Rolodex has tens of thousands of names and is electronically managed and supported by my team, so people connected to me are constantly being served and getting added value from me.

I've taken all three of these valuable pieces of life and business advice and proved them out to yet another generation. My two daughters (both young adults at the time of this publication) have begun to live these out daily in obvious ways that really make my wife and me proud.

My Father's Advice

by Jay Rodgers

Throughout my business career, I've had dozens of partners, fellow shareholders, and investors. In the multitude of entrepreneurial ventures that I've played a key role in, advice that my father gave me early on has stood me in great stead in building my business relationships. Because of that advice, I've enjoyed these relationships; and they have been virtually free of disagreement and conflict. His advice was simply that if you want to have a highly successful and congenial 50/50 partnership, be sure you enter that partnership mentally and emotionally prepared and willing to contribute 70 percent of the effort. Although the ratios were rarely 50/50, his advice applied to all my business relationships.

Following that guidance, I made it a practice to put more at risk than any of the other participants in any of my ventures. Despite the fact that I was active in managing most of the ventures and my fellow investors were passive, I took no compensation for the time and effort I supplied. I invested on a dollar-for-dollar basis with the passive investors and received no additional equity for having created and organized the venture.

When you read the final story of this book, you may better understand the true value of my father's advice. His advice provided me with an extremely enjoyable and successful career.

Paid Professional Advisors

Advisors like attorneys, CPAs, or financial planners who are hired based on their expertise in various areas are paid professional advisors. Their advice is essential in that some options require their input and knowledge in order for you to make the right decisions.

Traditionally, most business people have a minimum of five types of paid business advisors:

- Attorneys
- CPAs or bookkeepers
- Insurance agents who understand all forms of insurance
- Wealth management advisors
- Real Estate brokers

The more successful you become, the more advisors you will need – maybe even several within the same genre. Both Jay and Tony use several CPAs, for example, and they both have specialty attorneys they use on an as-needed basis – like a trust attorney, a deal attorney, a patent attorney, and a general attorney.

Remember, unless these advisors are successful entrepreneurs in their own right, the scope of their advice should be restricted to the knowledge and experience they bring in the areas of their expertise. You pay them to document and/or evaluate the facts and figures and point out to you the opportunities, challenges, and other ramifications involved in the various choices that are available to you, *not* to make decisions for you. And even if the advisors you choose are qualified by their own business success to make recommendations, the final decision is yours.

There are other kinds of paid professional advisors, though, from whom we *do* often seek recommendations. For example, Tony has advisors to help him with his books, like his literary agent Larry Carpenter, who gives Tony the benefit of his valuable expertise in the publishing world. And we all have health advisors like doctors and dentists, and sometimes nutritionists and trainers. We want to point out here that when we pursue advice from health advisors, it's imperative that we do the same due diligence we would for any other advisors: research their background and track record, get referrals, and determine how they've helped other people. It is best, if possible, to seek advice from those we already know and trust, or at least from those who have been referred by someone who has complete confidence in them. Even then, there will be times we should seek second opinions – as in serious health situations. (Remember, there are some bad advisors out there, and it's up to you to find the Master advisors in any situation, including your health.) Health is such an overlooked area where the *right* advisors can really make an impact. Believe it or not, Tony has about a dozen advisors in this area alone because of his personal commitment to health as well as his desire to learn and share with his clients, most of whom share his goal of ultimate health.

Remember to do your homework before you hire *any* advisors. The best scenario is to hire those referred to you by trusted friends or colleagues who have already established a relationship with them. Even if they are referred to you, be sure to look at their track record, their level of past successes, and their trustworthiness. Interview them, and talk to some of their major clients; read any testimonials they may have on the web; and Google them. If possible, avoid having to find a paid advisor on the spur of the moment without the benefit of research or referral. You may recall that Jay put a note on his calendar to find the right mergers and acquisitions attorney two years before the date he had marked on his calendar to sell Healthcare Staff Resources. You will appreciate the value of working with someone you trust when the time comes.

> Tony travels to Europe to see one of the best, or perhaps the world's top endocrinologist. Dr. Thierry Hertoghe is a fourth-generation hormone replacement therapy physician in Brussels. Go for the best!

And we cannot over-emphasize the importance of choosing paid advisors who are extremely successful in their fields. Tony doesn't hire unhealthy trainers. He hires those who practice what they teach and who have reached an extraordinary level of success in training others to be healthy. In the same vein, he doesn't go to unhealthy doctors. He chooses those who live a healthy lifestyle and are highly successful in keeping their patients healthy. Again, do your homework. Make sure you see in the advisors you choose the level of results you want for yourself.

RESOURCES

There are, of course, many excellent resources out there, such as books, videos, audios, and URL's, that can give you the benefit of someone else's findings from years of study and experience. The great thing here is that the advice from these resources is available in unlimited quantity, for an unlimited period of time, and at little or no cost.

Both Tony and Jay have read and studied literally thousands of books over the years, and they have had a huge impact on their lives and success. (Email info@tonyjeary.com and request your free copy of his Top 100 Books list.) The beautiful thing about it is, anyone can impact someone else's life simply by handing them an excellent book that will give them the insights they may need.

Tony keeps a list of the books he's read; and he has his staff make what he calls "Tony's Cliff Notes" from the books so he can have them at his fingertips and refer to them in a matter of minutes to find the advice he needs – even from books he read decades ago. He also has these Cliff Notes as part of his arsenal of resources, and he shares them with his clients as added value.

"YOU MUST READ TO LEAD. READING FEEDS. IT OPENS OUR SOULS TO A LONG LINE OF COUNSELORS."— *AM I CALLED?: THE SUMMONS TO PASTORAL MINISTRY*

You may not have thought about the benefit of collecting URLs. Tony has a list of dozens of URLs that he (or his clients) can go to for powerful videos and helpful advice any time. Those URLs are ever-living portals that keep people updated on just about any topic he discusses. For example, he has on his list URLs that can analyze your website for you. He keeps this list on his phone so he can access it any time. He also has a list of remarkable YouTube videos he's found that make great points, including some that may be used to jazz up a presentation or drive home a point he is making.

Early in his career, when he was still in his 20s, Tony attended an SMI (Success Motivation Institute) event, and they had all of their audio library on sale for about 80% off! He told the lady behind the table that he wanted one of everything. She was shocked! In fact, she thought she had heard him wrong and asked him to repeat his request. He invested several thousand dollars that day, and he says it was one of the best investments he has ever made. He had heard an author share that if you studied a subject for 30 minutes a day for a year, you would become an expert on that subject. He thought, "What if I study success and results for an hour a day for the rest of my life? Where will that lead me?" So he's done just that. He started by listening to Paul Myers and hundreds of other powerful authorities on those audios over and over for years, until he almost had some of them memorized. Those audios had a huge impact on helping him design the life he wanted. He also studied personal development gurus of that time, including Ken Blanchard, Stephen Covey, Zig Ziglar, and Brian Tracy. Since then, he has continued studying success principles through books, audios, videos, YouTube, Ted Talks, and anything else of strong value he can find. It works.

YOURSELF (SELF-REFLECTION)

We believe that another vital source of advice is self-reflection. It's so important to reflect on what's gone right or wrong in your own life and business, and what you need to improve on. This includes any decisions you've made and the principles that are on your *Belief Window*. For example, if Tony is listening to an audio recording of a book like *How to Win Friends and Influence People* and it says something like, "Use people's names," he might stop and think, "Well, I do use people's names, but I don't do it as much as I should." So he makes a choice; he decides to change or update that principle on his window and live that out more as part of his daily standards.

Reflecting on what has gone right in your life helps reinforce the good decisions and habits that led to that success. In Tony's goal-setting book, *Designing Your Own Life*, he recommends that his readers capture and celebrate their accomplishments, which serves as inspiration and motivation to continue moving forward. It's a great way to find value in the things you have done, as well as to validate the values you live by.

Self-talk is very effective as you reflect on the things you need to improve on. You know from your experience that there is a better way, so you can tell yourself, "In the future, do this."

You may remember the conference table we talked about in the Introduction, which doubles as an elaborate light fixture in Jay's office. It also doubles as a channel for his self-reflection. On the top of the glass table, he has etched the logos of most of the companies he has successfully run and sold for millions. But there's one logo that's embedded in a storm cloud, with lightning coming out of one end and an ugly face on the other. That represents one of the biggest mistakes he made in his career. Ironically, it's the company that produced the four cylinders that stabilize the table/light fixture as it moves from the table top to the ceiling. The way he figures it, those four cylinders cost him about $50,000 or $60,000 apiece, because they are the only things he walked away with. The point Jay made by putting that icon on the table top is this: Don't try to hide your mistakes. Think back on them and learn from them. If you happen to visit Jay's office and visit the lavatory, you may wonder about a painting on the wall showing a four-hitch chuck wagon going over a cliff. That's a reminder to Jay of another one of his mistakes.

For quick reference, we have prepared the matrix below showing the six sources of advice and a short description of each:

The Six Sources of Advice

Source	Description
Coach	A paid professional who challenges and inspires you to be your best, reach your goals, overcome your weaknesses, and grow your strengths through structured, one-on-one sessions. A great coach will help you advance your career, grow your leadership skills, build your brand, and uncover *Blind Spots*. A Master coach will also help you gain strategic clarity, develop focused plans, and execute more effectively.
Mentor	A person you have identified through your connections who is extremely successful and is willing to invest in your life, free of charge, by sharing in informal meetings his or her successes and mistakes in order to have an impact on the decisions you make. A mentor is often a veteran in your field or has been somewhere you want to go and can keep you from experiencing pitfalls. Ideally, a mentor is someone who is strong in the areas where you know you are weak.
Trusted Colleagues (Including Family)	People in your life whom you relate to, admire, and trust enough to trade off some of your advice for their advice. They may be people who have demonstrated an ability to think beyond the way most people think. They could be clients, co-workers, friends, or family, but you respect the way they see the world, what they've done, and the successes they've had.
Paid Professional Advisors	Advisors like attorneys, CPAs or bookkeepers, insurance agents, and financial planners who are hired based on their expertise and success in various areas. Their advice is essential in the sense that you need their knowledge in order to make great decisions. They could also be health advisors – like doctors, dentists, nutritionists, and trainers – or any other professionals you pay for advice.
Resources	Sources of information like books, videos, audios, and URL's. These sources can give you the benefit of someone else's findings from years of study and experience.
Yourself (Self-Reflection)	Reflecting on successes and areas that need improvement. This includes decisions you've made, the principles that are on your *Belief Window*, and your successes and mistakes.

V.I.P.s

- Your chances of success increase exponentially when you seek the advice of others who are already extremely successful and are willing to invest in your life by sharing their experiences and learned success principles.

- One-on-one coaching can advance your career, grow your leadership skills, help you build your brand, and uncover *Blind Spots*. The right coach can take you to the next level, where you see a significant increase in your income, reach your goals faster, and become stronger in all areas of your life.

- A mentor is often a veteran in your field or has been somewhere you want to go and can keep you from experiencing pitfalls that he or she may or may not have avoided. Ideally, a mentor is someone who is strong in the areas where you know you are weak.

- As you go through life, you often find people you relate to and admire, and you may bounce things off of each other. Those people are not really coaches or mentors; they are colleagues or family members that you trust and look up to for advice. You respect the way they see the world, what they've done, and the successes they've had.

- The advice of paid professional advisors is essential in the sense that you need their knowledge in order to make great decisions. Even if the paid professional advisors you choose are qualified by their own success as an entrepreneur to make recommendations, it's up to you to consider your options and make the business decisions yourself.

- Remember to do your homework before you hire any advisors. Even if they are referred to you, be sure to research their track record.

- There are many excellent resources out there, such as books, videos, audios, and URL's, that can give you the benefit of someone else's findings from years of study and experience.

- It's important to reflect on what's gone right or wrong in your own life and business, and what you need to improve on. This includes any decisions you've made and the principles that are on your *Belief Window*.

Chapter 3

Gathering Your Advisors

Henry Ford once filed a libel lawsuit against a Chicago newspaper for calling him "an ignorant pacifist." In an attempt to prove their point in court, the attorneys for the newspaper asked Mr. Ford a series of questions, none of which he could answer correctly. Finally tiring of their game, Mr. Ford pointed his finger at the lawyer who had asked most of the questions, and said, in essence, that he had a row of buttons on his desk and could push any one of them at any time to call someone on his staff who could answer any question he would ever need to ask. The point of that story, of course, is that you are wise, indeed, to surround yourself with people who know more than you do in the areas where you need help. Or, put even more simply, you are wise in proportion to your collective advisory team.

Jack Welch, the legendary chairman and CEO of General Electric who increased the company's value by 4,000 percent during his 20-year tenure, obviously agreed. "From the first person I hired, I was never the smartest guy in the room," Welch said. "And that's a big deal. And if you're going to be a leader - if you're a leader and you're the smartest guy… in the room, you've got real problems."

These two men epitomized the principle that *advice matters*. If two of the most successful business people in the world felt it absolutely essential to surround themselves with individuals who could give them the benefit of their wisdom, expertise, insights, and knowledge, don't you think that practice could help you reach new heights of success, as well?

The Two Most Important Things to Remember When Gathering Your Advisors

Douglas Adams, an English writer, humorist, and dramatist, once said, "The quality of any advice anybody has to offer has to be judged against the quality of life they actually lead." Remember the *Mastery Impact Curve* graphic in Chapter 1 that showed the coinciding rise of quality of advice and results? Bad, good, and great advice leads to bad, good, and great results, respectively. If you want results on the Mastery level, though, you must get Mastery advice. That means whether you're looking for a coach, a mentor, an attorney, or even a book, you want the best – Mastery – so you can get Mastery results.

The first thing to remember when you are gathering your advisors is to make sure those you select know what they're talking about. Do your prospective advisors just have academia, which only qualifies them to point you to a book; or do they have expertise and history, with the track record of results you want to see in your own life and business? Do they have their failures well documented so they can help you avoid them? Have they been where you want to go and achieved the success you want to achieve? Your life and career are far too valuable to trust them to someone who is not qualified to give you exceptional advice.

> **"THE QUALITY OF ANY ADVICE ANYBODY HAS TO OFFER HAS TO BE JUDGED AGAINST THE QUALITY OF LIFE THEY ACTUALLY LEAD."**
>
> **—DOUGLAS ADAMS**

Actually, your job is not to find advisors; it's to find *outstanding* advisors. Does that sound like a lot of work? It is, because you have to do your research to make sure you find winners. You must use selective criteria to find the right advisors. Validate the potential value the advisors can provide to you by interviewing them and others they've helped (major clients, mentees, etc.), reading testimonials of what they've done for others, and finding out anything else you can about them to see if their advising modality matches what works for you. Have they achieved the kind of results you're looking for? If you're considering a coach, does he or she have a powerful mind and a research arsenal that could benefit you? If you're considering a book, is it just a collection of stories, or does it give you a checklist or a model you can immediately use? When you're looking at any of the six sources of advice, you want them to be able to bring what they have to the table in a way that you can use it.

Remember, your advisors are just that – advisors. Even if the advice they give is the best in the world, the final decisions you make in your life and business are still yours and yours alone. Jay and Tony have a fantastic reciprocal relationship; Jay has been Tony's mentor for many years and Tony has coached Jay on business matters. As much as they respect and admire each other, and as much as they value and appreciate the advice they receive from each other, they still leave the table knowing the final decisions are theirs. Whether they decide to apply 20 percent, 80 percent, or 100 percent of the advice they receive from each other, it's their choice. In fact, Jay tells the people

YOUR LIFE AND CAREER ARE FAR TOO VALUABLE TO TRUST THEM TO SOMEONE WHO IS NOT QUALIFIED TO GIVE YOU EXCEPTIONAL ADVICE.

he mentors, "I can give you the world's greatest advice on how to achieve something; but if my recommendations don't fit you mentally – if they just don't feel right to you – then don't take my advice."

Steven, the CEO of Rhino Fleet Tracking, a GPS tracking company Jay founded, disagrees. He suggests that if the advice doesn't fit or doesn't feel right, save it for future consideration rather than throwing it out. It took him a long time to digest Jay's out-of-the-box approaches and become comfortable with them. He had been listening to Jay's stories of creative deal structuring for a couple of years when he had an opportunity to respond to a request for proposal from a Fortune 100 company. By the time Steven put the proposal together, he firmly believed in Jay's conviction that the best way to win big was to spend your time helping your customers achieve their goals. While doing his due diligence for the proposal, Steven became convinced that the company's executives wanted a partner to teach them the business; and as soon as they achieved a significant volume, they would take the entire project in-house.

All of Steven's competitors proposed providing a turnkey take-it-or-leave-it solution. Steven's proposal was multi-layered. He offered to provide all services in the beginning; then, as the volume grew and it made economic sense, he would train their personnel and turn over various portions of the project. By that time, Rhino's proprietary software would be an integral part of the program. Therefore, it would be preferable to license it and pay Rhino a reoccurring fee based on volume, rather than replacing it. Steven's proposal made long-term economic sense for both companies and created an ongoing strategic partnership. Rhino Fleet Tracking was awarded the contract.

When Steven reviewed the contract with attorney David Hammer, David commented, "It just takes a little bit to understand these creative deals Jay puts together."

Steven replied, "Well, thank you. That was actually a clause I put together."

David responded, "You've been hanging out with Jay too much!"

The second extremely important marker to look for is alignment of values. It is critical to choose advisors whose values line up with your own personal values. What are the top ten things that are most important to you and that drive your life? Honesty? Faith? Health? Philanthropy? Knowledge? Personal Brand? Results? Time? Creativity? Most people haven't taken the time to reflect on what their real values are. (Email info@tonyjeary.com for a complimentary list of 60 values to sort from.) Identifying your true values will give you the great clarity you need when you're sizing up your potential advisors, to make sure you are both heading in the same direction. The last thing you want are advisors who will influence you to go where you don't want to go or clash with what you deem important. Moving you out of your comfort zone, however, is an entirely different matter; and that's a great thing, as long as the move is in the right direction and it doesn't compromise your values.

Here is an example of what that looks like. Tony realized years ago that one of his values was maximizing time and energy. He also valued having more time with his family. So he closed the offices he had set up around the world and built a unique, second-to-none private studio on his estate in the DFW area. Now, most of his clients fly in from all over the world to meet with him there, and he gets to work from his back yard – maximizing time and energy and giving him more time with his family. The relative aspect of this story, though, is that he looks for advisors who align with this value. Rather than spending time and energy going to see his CPA of 25-plus years, David Boden (a paid professional advisor), for example, he has his CPA come to his studio. And Jay shares that same value, so he looks for paid professional advisors who are willing to come to his office, as well. In fact, most of the meetings he attends with his paid advisors or mentees, as well as planning and board meetings for Biz Owners Ed and Rhino Fleet Tracking, are held in his office.

Please understand that this is just an example. We realize that having your paid professional advisors come to you may not be a priority for you, although it might be if one of your top values is maximizing time and energy. There is no absolute, here; that just happens to be a value of top importance for us, and it makes for a great working relationship when the people who bring their expertise to the table for us are in alignment. When we are interviewing our paid advisors, one of the things we look for is whether they will fit with that value and, consequently, our way of doing business.

YOUR JOB IS NOT TO FIND ADVISORS; IT'S TO FIND *OUTSTANDING* ADVISORS.

Along the same vein, Jim Norman, the coach Tony had for decades, shared his value of time efficiency. Several years ago he came to Tony and said, "Listen, what you really want is just my advice when you need it, and you know you can call me seven days a week. Why don't I just charge you by the minute, rather than blocking off hours for us to meet?" Jim said, "Anytime you need me, you just call me. Whether you want me to read something or watch something, or you want to talk to me on the phone or have me come to your studio, I'll just send you a bill each month for however many minutes I poured into you." It's very unusual for a coach to think like that, and it fit Tony's values perfectly! The point is, without alignment of your *values*, you won't get maximum *value* from your advisors.

We've talked a lot about "values" and "value" here – one is the standards you live your life by and the other is the worth of your advisors, in terms of what they can bring to you. Both are critical to your success.

When you're choosing any of these six sources of advice, you want to find those who will bring what they have to you in the way that you can use it best. So how do you find the right advisors? Since we are both asked that question often, we want to spend the rest of this chapter further exploring how to find those advisors that can bring maximum value to you.

COACHES

How do you find the right coach? What kind of value should you look for?

For 30 years, Tony has advised, coached, and guided many of the world's top business organizations. He has done this with an unprecedented commitment to gathering, organizing, cataloging, and developing results-oriented business resources to utilize for his special clients. He selects from this treasure chest of resources daily to enhance his clients' thinking, clarify their vision, impact their *Belief Window*, focus their planning, and accelerate the execution of the results they desire.

Few coaches have been as intentional as Tony has been for decades to collect and organize such a complete array of tools to have at their fingertips. It all started in the early 90s when he was working as a tier-two supplier for eight major advertising agencies, including Bozell, OmniCom, BBDO, Imagination out of London, and others. He realized that these agencies weren't disciplined in organizing all of their best practices. Tony believed that if he was disciplined and if he could sort and organize all the best practices of all the projects and clients he worked with over the decades, he could one day have an arsenal no one else in the world would have. And that's exactly what he did. He now has tools on how to brand and how to merchandise, courses on time management, and tools to assist in addressing almost any challenge or opportunity his client encounters.

Now, when Tony's clients mention a challenge, he has at his fingertips exactly what they need. Recently, he had clients in his studio who said their biggest issue was delegation. He responded, "I've written a book called *How to Gain 100 Extra Minutes a Day*, and 25 percent of that book is on delegation. I've summarized the book on one page; and I will not only give you the book, but I will also give you the page that summarizes it all."

We believe that any Master coach will have an arsenal of organized content to bring to the table, which will include documented business acumen, models, processes, publications, articles, software, courses, marketing tools, presentation tools, and personal improvement tools. He or she will then draw from that arsenal only those items that precisely apply to your specific situation. The extraordinary coach will also have a giant Rolodex full of contacts, and he or she will have done favors in advance for many of those contacts in order to build *Trust Transference*. Then, in many cases, the coach can pull the precise contact who will be able help you fulfill whatever need you may have at the time.

A coach's value really comes from the results he or she brings. Remember, the right coach is an investment – not an expense – because a coach will dramatically alter the results of your life.

Tony has stayed fully booked for many years; and at this point in his life he's simply focused on selecting people to work with who are dedicated to winning. He read a book by Gerry Spence, an attorney in Wyoming, called *How to Argue and Win Every Time*. Tony was fascinated that Spence had never lost a case. He thought, "How in the world could you be an attorney for three decades and never lose a case?" He discovered the answer in the book: You just take on cases you know you can win. So now he's very selective about who he takes on as a client, because at this stage of his life he loves to work with winners. In fact, when he's choosing his clients, he selects only those clients who qualify according to his ADOME model:

A – Aggressive

D – Desire to do business with Tony

O – Open Minded

M – Money. His coaching can produce significant financial gain for his clients

E – Equity play. Bonus payout options in stock or other, based on the results he gets as the relationship grows

Before Tony agrees to work with a new client, he conducts a mutual interview. He wants to make sure the client will be happy with him, and he wants to ensure that the client is a winner who fits his ADOME model. He sometimes suggests that a client hire him for a small assignment so they can *both* see if there is a fit before they get into a long-term relationship.

And that's another characteristic you want to look for when you are evaluating a coach: Be sure you get one that's selective about who he or she coaches. Most of the time, a Master coach will only work with those whose desire to win is strong enough to compel them to do whatever it takes to produce a win. The coach who has no criteria for selecting clients is probably the wrong coach for you.

MENTORS

How do you find the right mentors who will be a good fit for you and will pour into you the wisdom and insight you need?

We suggest that you search among your own contacts and use all of the networking opportunities available to you to find the right mentors. It's critical that you find people who have done or are doing what you want to do. You may find people who are the best at what they do, but are they the best at doing *what you need*? In other words, make sure you don't get an expert ear doctor to do open heart surgery – and that applies to all of your advisors, whether they are coaches, mentors, trusted colleagues, or paid professional advisors. Don't just seek out experts, but seek out experts who are important to you and your goals.

Here's another important point about finding a mentor: You may want to look for a mentor who is in your industry, but who is not in your market. In so doing, you could be more successful in finding a powerful mentor who may enjoy helping someone climb the ladder in the same business that he or she understands so well, since the mentor does not see you as a competitor from the same market.

Jay has mentored hundreds of people over his lifetime; many of them are people he had never met until they asked for his help. Recently, a young woman was referred to Jay by a good friend, who is also a business partner and a psychiatrist. The young woman called to schedule an appointment with Jay, and he had never heard anyone sound as depressed, despondent, and discouraged as this young lady. Because his friend had referred her, Jay invited her to come out to his office that afternoon. When she arrived, the look on her face would have frightened even an undertaker.

She explained that the general manager of her cupcake company and one of her key operational people had recently walked out without notice. After talking to her for some time, Jay was convinced that she was an outstanding marketer and salesperson for her company, but she had no desire or aptitude for the operational aspects. The business had grown and was now beyond her aspiration or ability to manage. The loss of her manager had simply been the catalyst that brought it all crashing down. Orders were not being delivered in a timely manner, the quality of their product had suffered, production had fallen to the point that they had stopped accepting B to B orders, and they were forced to close their retail store early each day.

Jay told her that, since his friend had referred her, he was willing to mentor her, but only if she fully understood and agreed to the following terms:

1. She should expect it to take at least six months to turn the company around, get it back on track, and make it profitable.
2. She had to be willing to spend $50,000-$60,000 in the process of restoring the business to profitability. (Fortunately, she had the funds available to do that, if necessary.)
3. She had to agree that the number one priority was to hire a competent general manager; and, in order to get the talent and experience necessary, she must be willing to pay her new manager about twice what her former manager had made.

She understood and accepted all three conditions. They then established the ground rules for their mentor/mentee relationship. Just 60 days after their first meeting, the mentee arrived for her scheduled meeting with Jay excited, smiling, and filled with good news:

1. Her new general manager had been on board for almost six weeks; he had taken charge and was doing a great job.
2. She was on target to return to profitability within the next 30 days.
3. She only had to put an additional $20,000 into the company since their first meeting, and she felt that that she would be able to achieve positive cash flow and profitability without adding any additional money.

There are still several issues that must be addressed, but the company is back on track and headed in the right direction. In just two months, Jay had helped her turn both her life and her business around!

ADVICE DOES MATTER!

Like Tony, Jay is very selective about who he works with. He made the decision many years ago that he wanted to help people, and he also decided he only wanted to work with those who really wanted to excel. In December 2007 the *Dallas CEO Magazine* (a division of *D Magazine*) did a feature article on Jay, billing him as a successful entrepreneur who has built and sold over a dozen companies and helped countless other business owners do the same. And the article mentioned that Jay, though "retired," continues to consult for small business owners – for free. A person who does that is called a mentor.

Jay, in fact, delights in helping entrepreneurs grow their companies. When the *Dallas CEO Magazine* article generated so many entrepreneurs seeking mentorship, it allowed Jay to select only those who had the desire, persistence, and commitment to win. That's when he decided to expand his efforts and start Biz Owners Ed. Behind all of his efforts is the sincere belief that the growth of small business means more jobs and more prosperity for our economy. Small business made our country the world's greatest nation and will keep us on top if it flourishes.

Remember the opening story in Chapter 1 about Claude and Alan? Those two met each other – and Jay – in 1990 at a three-year Owner/President Management program at Harvard Business School designed for small entrepreneurial companies (less than $100 million in revenue). There were 86 participants in their class, from around 30 different countries. Though the lessons learned in the class were valuable, Jay felt that he gained the most value from the peer group interchange. Alan would probably agree, since it was a relationship that came out of that school that gained advice that helped him grow his company by several billion dollars. So when you consider investing your time and money to attend schools, seminars, conventions, trade shows, or any other networking event, you might want to think about the sharp people you could meet there who may be able to give you advice and help you make better decisions. If you attend with that specific goal in mind, you'll be more attuned to finding the right people to help you. And when you find them, don't be afraid to ask! If you don't ask, they can't say yes.

Jay served on a grand jury recently, and a fellow juror approached him about helping her with her business. He knew they had one mutual friend, but he was puzzled as to why she would ask him. "Three people have suggested I should get you to help me," she explained. (Now that's a great example of using all of your networking opportunities – even serving on a jury – to find mentors!) At that point, her business was 23 years old, and for the last three years she had been losing money. She had reached the point where she didn't even want to get up and go to work each day. Jay's first advice to her was to raise all of her prices 20 percent. Although she feared she would be priced out of the market and lose all of her customers, she took his advice. She lost a couple of customers; but that 20 percent went straight to the bottom line, and it got her quickly into the black. With just that one piece of advice, Jay was able to help save her company, and then he went on to help her with what she said were valuable suggestions.

Once you have done your research and you find someone you would like to have as a mentor, we recommend that you go into the relationship informally and don't establish a long-term relationship or agreement until you find out if you fit each other and are comfortable. You might have lunch, get acquainted, and ask for help on a small scale. Don't jump in and try to set up a year-long or lifelong mentor/mentee relationship until you ease into it pretty informally, and then grow the relationship.

PAID PROFESSIONAL ADVISORS

How do you find the best paid professional advisors that fit your needs?

Everything we've said so far applies to finding the right paid professional advisors, as well as coaches and mentors. Get referrals, use all of your contacts and networking opportunities, and keep your eyes open for the best of the best. When you find them, look at testimonials, find out what kind of reputation they have in the business world and community, talk to people they have already advised, do an Internet search for them, and find out anything else you can to help validate the additional energy that you will be pouring into a relationship.

We want to remind you again that when choosing paid advisors like attorneys or CPAs, you want to take advice in proportion to their true expertise and experience. Even if these people may be the very best at what they do, unless they have a proven track record of success as an entrepreneur, they are to only give you facts, figures, and the consequences of the various courses of action available to you. They are usually coming from a completely different mindset than an entrepreneur or a top executive; it is your life, your business, and your reward. The final decision is on your shoulders and is for you alone to make.

TRUSTED COLLEAGUES (INCLUDING FAMILY)

Where do you find trusted colleagues?

Trusted colleagues are people you already know, whom you trust and can relate to, and who are willing to trade advice with you. You can find trusted colleagues anywhere you are doing life. They may be people that you already bounce business ideas off of; they may serve on a board or a committee with you; they may be from your small group at church; or they may be your neighbor, your client, your family member, or your best friend. A trusted colleague is often someone who has demonstrated an ability to think beyond most people's thinking. You respect them for the way they see the world and – like your other advisors – you admire what they've done and the successes they've had.

RESOURCES

Powerful advice can and should come into your life through books, audios, videos, and other learning tools. So, how do you find the right resources that will give you the best advice in the areas where you need to grow?

A really good standard to go by when considering resources is endorsement. When a certain book or video is a hot topic among the successful people you know, for example, or when one or more of your advisors recommends a resource to you because he or she knows you and believes it will be helpful to you, it's probably worth investing your time in. Tony and Jay both go after referrals when they are selecting resources, because they don't want to put their valuable time into something that's not extremely pertinent to their success.

Referrals are a great starting point for gathering resources. Again, we recommend validating the value of the advice you can get from that resource, even if it is referred.

The best resources will often contain simple models that you can take away and apply to your life. When you start to read a book, for example, make sure it's not just a collection of stories and that it makes you think and/or it gives you information you can use. If not, ask yourself if you really want to invest valuable study time. Be intentional; build systems and habits that ensure your are getting extraordinary resources coming into your life.

Yourself (Self-Reflection)

How can you best use self-reflection as a dynamic source of advice?

The main thing you need to remember here is that you have to give yourself time to reflect on the things that have worked, the things that haven't, and the things you need to improve on. If you don't build "thinking time" into your schedule, you'll miss out on the incredible benefits of the clarity it brings.

Tony teaches his clients the power of thinking and suggests they strategically build thinking into their daily High Leverage Activities (HLAs). He was recently working with a CEO of a billion-dollar public company who asked Tony to encourage his executives to do just that. He had come to believe so strongly in the power of calculated thinking that he wanted to change the culture of the entire company to incorporate the concept of thinking as an HLA. Thinking and reflecting is a powerful tool that will yield outstanding advice; and if you don't put it into your schedule, you will often get too busy to leave time for it.

Which Advisors are Right for You?

As you're considering the advisors you need to gather around you, your first action should be to sit down and do an honest evaluation of where your greatest needs are in the categories of coaches, mentors, trusted colleagues, and paid professional advisors, in both your personal and professional life. This will give you an idea of who you're looking for.

For example, there are 120 trees on Tony's estate, in a gorgeous park-like setting; so one of the personal advisors he needs is a horticulturist. If Tony has a problem with a plant, he can take a picture of its leaf and text it to his horticulturist, who can tell him right away what the problem is and what to do about it. Jay has no need for a horticulturist; he does, however, need a veterinarian to help him take care of his horses, because horses are a big part of his life.

Everyone has different needs. If you're a corporate executive, you'll need someone to help you negotiate your compensation package and support your strategic vision. If you're an entrepreneur, your priority may be to have an exceptional deal attorney and tax counsel to help you raise money and put deals together. Think about your life, both personal and professional, analyze your weaknesses and your needs, and determine what kind of advice you need to help you do life better. Then make sure you have outstanding advisors to support those areas of your life.

Here's a template with examples following that will hopefully jog your thinking as you're considering the different strengths you need in all the different categories of advisors to help you be your very best. These are just a few of the hundreds of possibilities, of course. As you read through the list, check off any that apply to your particular needs; and then use it as a springboard to help you think of other advisors who could help you.

Source	Purpose
Coach	
Mentor	
Trusted Colleagues (Including Family)	
Paid Professional Advisors	

Example:

Source	Purpose
Coach	Life Coach
	Business Strategist
	Presentation Coach
	Sports Coach (for you or your kids)
	College coach (to help your kids find the right college)
	Music Coach
	Driving Coach
	Language Coach
Mentor	Business
	Marriage
	Spiritual
	Parenting
	Health
Trusted Colleagues (Including Family)	Business
	Life (any area you have a need)
Paid Professional Advisors	General Attorney
	Deal Attorney
	Patent Attorney
	Trust Attorney
	CPA
	Bookkeeper
	Financial Advisor
	Insurance Broker
	Real Estate Broker
	Doctor
	Dentist
	Trainer
	Nutritionist
	Horticulturist
	Expert Mechanic
	Photographer
	Videographer
	Graphic Designer
	Ghostwriter/Editor
	Literary Agent
	Publisher
	Veterinarian

As you go through this list, think about the areas of your life where you would like to have people around you who know more than you do and can pour into your life in those areas. Do you need a coach who will help you overcome your weaknesses, grow your strengths, and reach the next level of success in your life and business? Do you have mentors who are supporting the priorities in your life, helping you explore the accuracy of your *Belief Window*, and sharing their wisdom and insight? Do you have trusted colleagues (including family members) with whom you can relate, who can support you with their advice? What types of paid advisors do you need? How many specialty attorneys? How many specialty CPAs?

Just ask yourself: "Is my investment of time and/or money going to increase my bottom line profits and/or success?" As a corporate executive, for example, you have a board that wants you to be extremely successful. The board wants you not to make mistakes; yet they're not hiring you to know it all – they're hiring you to get the job done. So even if you have outstanding expertise with maybe three and four companies, do you have the knowledge base to do everything perfectly, versus a coach who has worked with hundreds of boards? Investing in a coach who will help you think of the things you should do and not miss any gaps is an extremely good investment for both you and the company.

And we don't want to discount the fact that you need to take advice from your own staff, as well. If you have an outstanding HR Director, or a Safety Director, or a Risk Director, for example, you may not need to hire outside people to advise you in those areas. What we are saying is that, as a leader, you need to look at your internal team as well as outside your team, and make sure you are gathering the people around you that really help you make the best things happen.

That applies on a personal basis, as well. In fact, we believe it's really helpful to departmentalize your advisors – that is, to seek wisdom and insight from people in different areas of your life who have successfully accomplished what you want to accomplish. If you want to have great kids, go to people who have great kids. If you want to have great health, seek advice from someone who is healthy. We mentioned in Chapter 2 that Tony and his wife have been able to raise incredible daughters; and he gives much credit to their mentors – families with exceptional daughters themselves who were about 10 years older than his – whom they went to for 20 years to gain discernment about what works and what doesn't.

Advice matters – not just in business, but in all of life. Like Tony, you may want help in the area of parenting your kids. You may need mentors to help you have an exceptional marriage. You may want someone to mentor you financially, or even spiritually. And life advisors are not limited to mentors. Just think how many paid advisors you use in the different areas of your life: an expert mechanic, a knowledgeable gardener or lawn specialist, a talented and highly trained hair specialist, and an experienced professional trainer, to name a few. If you find the right advisors, these people can be invaluable assets in helping you reach for the level of Mastery in everything you do.

Let's look at some examples: Tony has an Austrian trainer who has been studying body-building for 20 years, and he knows just about everything there is to know about the body. If he doesn't know, he'll find out. He can answer almost any question Tony can throw out – exactly how to warm up, how to keep from getting hurt, etc. – because he's already experienced most of the mistakes that can be made. He has the knowledge, the experience, and the success to qualify as a Master advisor in the area of training. When he says, "Don't drink this shake; drink this one," Tony has the confidence that he knows what he's talking about.

A while back, Tony was driving down the road, and he noticed that his car was shimmying slightly. He couldn't tell if it was the tires or if the car was out of alignment. Tony's personal driver, Roland, happens to be an auto hobbyist with a big garage on his property where he tinkers with his collection of cars. He's not only an auto expert; he's also a really good mechanic. So Roland took Tony's car; and when he came back, he explained in minute detail that the problem was due to the towing percentage required by Mercedes SLs because of the lightness of the car. The point is, Roland is the expert advisor; and Tony doesn't have to invest his time, energy, and brain power to figure out the problem.

Having expert advisors all around you frees you up to focus on the things that really matter, because then you don't have to know everything about everything. Jay and Tony don't study the IRS codes, with all of its endless changes. They have CPAs they keep on retainer to do that. When you surround yourself with exceptional advisors who are willing to apply their knowledge to your unique needs, you are both big winners.

There are even times when you can find exceptional advice where you least expect it. You may have heard the story of the truck that got stuck under the underpass and everyone around was trying to figure out how to get it out. A little boy sitting on a nearby curb said, "Why don't you let some air out of the tires?"

Jay likes to tell this story about Ford Motor Company: Many years ago, Ford was building a specific sedan model at three different plants, and they started getting reports that the front windshield on a particular model was leaking during moderate to heavy rains. As they started investigating, they determined that most of the problems were coming from two of the three plants. And when they looked deeper, they found that the cars that were being built by the night shift at the third plant had no problems. An engineering team flew down to the third plant to talk to the night supervisor. The team leader said, "We want to know how you put the front windshield in." The night supervisor said, "Well, we take some of the adhesive that we use to put the gaskets in the doors, and we apply it to the rubber frame for the front windshield. Then we put the windshield in the bottom and pop it into the top." The head engineer said, "You know, you're supposed to use the adhesive we formulated especially for the windshield, instead of the gasket adhesive. And the book clearly states that you're supposed to pop the top in and then the bottom." The foreman responded, "Well, yes; but if

EVEN IF YOU HAVE OUTSTANDING EXPERTISE WITH MAYBE THREE AND FOUR COMPANIES, DO YOU HAVE THE KNOWLEDGE BASE TO DO EVERYTHING PERFECTLY, VERSUS A COACH WHO HAS WORKED WITH HUNDREDS OF BOARDS?

ADVICE MATTERS

you do, it will leak." Sometimes you can get outstanding advice from the most unexpected places.

Ford has obviously come a long way in the matter of finding outstanding advice since then, as they've hired Tony to coach their president and sought his advice in many projects over the years. One day in 1995 someone from their top management called him and said, "We want you to help us with a team-building exercise for 180 of our top executives." Tony said, "Well, I'm not a team-building expert." The executive said, "We will pay you a million dollars," and Tony quickly responded, "Then I'll become a team-building expert!" They gave him the contract because of his track record of study and execution. They wanted someone they could trust. He went out and studied team-building and became the expert they needed.

Successful people constantly keep their eyes on the bottom line, both in business and in life. They ask, "Is what I'm doing working, or do I need help?" Having the *right* advisors in your life can bring incredible bottom-line increases in every area of your life, both personally and professionally.

67

V. I. P. s

- The first thing to remember when you are gathering your advisors is to make sure those you select know what they're talking about. Do your prospective advisors have the actual experience with the track record of results you want to see in your own life and business?

- Your job is not to find advisors; it's to find *outstanding* advisors.

- It is critical to choose advisors whose values line up with your own personal values.

- When you're choosing any of the six sources of advice, you want to find those who will bring what they have to the table for you in the way that you can use it best.

- A Master coach will bring an arsenal of organized content to the table and will draw from that arsenal only those items that precisely apply to the client's specific situation.

- Search among your own contacts and use all of the networking opportunities available to you to find the right mentors. You may find people who are the best at what they do, but are they the best at doing *what you need*?

- A really good standard to go by when considering resources is endorsement. When a certain book or video is a hot topic among the successful people you know, for example, or when one or more of your advisors recommends a resource to you because he or she knows you and believes it will be helpful to you, it's probably worth investing your time in.

- Give yourself time to reflect on the things that have worked, the things that haven't, and the things you need to improve on. If you don't build "thinking time" into your schedule, you'll miss out on the incredible benefits of the clarity it brings.

CHAPTER 4

THE FOUR-STEP PROCESS FOR GETTING ADVICE

"He that won't be counseled can't be helped."
–BENJAMIN FRANKLIN

A venture capitalist and one of Tony's colleagues recently approached him about leveraging his brand to help them launch a particular entity, and Tony was very intrigued with their proposal. As the discussion started to get a little complicated, Tony said, "For us to go to the next step, we need my deal attorney. We need someone to help us put the whole deal together. David Hammer is both a CPA and an attorney who has closed over 150 major M&A transactions. He can not only help me figure out my piece to the puzzle; he can also help us determine the type of entity we need to set up and help us structure the deal as we're bringing in all the different partners." Tony asked the other two principal players to schedule a time to meet with David, interview him, and validate what he had said about him. They did, and they were very impressed with David and happy with Tony for suggesting they bring him in. David, who is a very successful entrepreneur in his own right, is, at the time of this writing, in the process of helping them sort out all of the pieces of the deal and formulating suggestions as to how to proceed. From that, they will weigh all of their options and make a decision as to how to go forward and put the deal together.

Advice matters. It is next to impossible to achieve the Master level of success without gleaning counsel from those who have the expertise, history, and experience to help take us where we want to go. Even with all the remarkable talents and accomplishments of Tony and his two associates combined, there was still a void in the knowledge and proficiency needed to put the right pieces together to accomplish their goals. Once they found the right person with the right advice, though, they were able to move forward with confidence and success.

In the above example, and in most every situation where decisions are to be made, you will find that there are four simple steps to help you navigate through the choices and options available for getting advice. These steps are pretty simple, and yet very valuable. To help you digest the progression, let's first look at the four-step process, and then we'll see how those steps played out in the illustration above.

Here is the four-step process for getting advice:

1. Identify your issues and opportunities. Look at where you are compared to where you want to be, and list the issues you're struggling with that are keeping you from crossing that gap. (Note: Your advisors may – and probably will – help you identify more issues and Blind Spots than you are able to identify at the beginning.) Make a list of the opportunities available to you, as well, so you can seek wisdom and input as to how (or whether) to move forward.

2. Determine the best resource(s) available to get advice. You may be just beginning to build your business or starting your career, or perhaps just realizing you need help in your personal life; if that's the case, you may want to start with trusted colleagues and a mentor or two until your revenue can support a coach. Don't wait too long on the coach option; consider that the right coach can steer you in the best direction, help you avoid catastrophic mistakes, and often give advice that brings in a huge payoff. A few recommendations could more than make up for the money you would invest by saving you time, increasing your return, and helping you avoid mistakes. Or your situation may call for choosing one or more paid advisors you can trust and who can give you Master advice. And also remember all of the resources (books, videos, URLs, etc.) available to you; consider investing as much time as you can studying as many resources as you can to learn as much as you can. And finally, be sure to devote time reflecting on your past experiences and learning from yourself.

3. Gather options or possible solutions from your advisor(s), and then review the plusses and minuses (including the risks). The buck stops with you. Listen to the suggestions served up by your coach, your mentor(s), your trusted colleagues, and/or your paid advisors; and list any ideas

or options you identified from your resources and self-reflection. Then carefully weigh all of the information and options you've gathered.

4. Take action accordingly. After careful consideration of all of your options, confidently choose the best path for you and go forward based on the advice of what, where, why, how, and when you received from your advisors. By going through this process, you will have catapulted your chances for success.

The Four-Step Process for Getting Advice

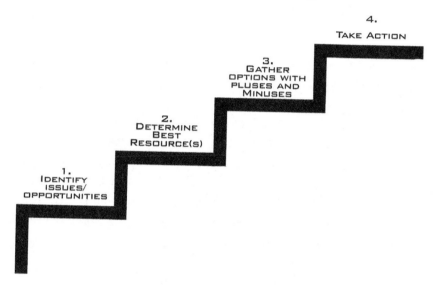

Step 1 is to identify the issue and the opportunities. In the opening illustration, the issue was actually twofold: First, they wanted to structure a relationship with a worldwide company. Second, they wanted to put together an organizational structure for the ownership of the investment entity they were forming. They had a goal, but there was a gap between where they were and the accomplishment of their goal – a knowledge of the legal and financial steps needed to get there. They needed advice from an expert who could fill that gap.

Step 2 is to determine the best resource to get that advice from. Through Tony's personal knowledge and experience with David Hammer and the added due diligence performed by the other two principal players, they determined that David was the best advisor for the job. His entrepreneurial success, along with his credentials as an excellent CPA and attorney, gave them confidence that he was the right person to help them sort out the possibilities.

Step 3 is to gather the options or possible solutions, and then review the plusses and minuses (including the risks). David is currently in the process of putting together a plan for the best way to structure the pieces. He will present his recommendations to Tony and his two associates, and they will then weigh out the advantages and risks of each suggestion.

Step 4 is take action. Once Tony and his partners agree on the best path to take, based upon the options presented to them by David Hammer, they will proceed accordingly with full knowledge of the ramifications of the actions they choose. By completing this four-step process, their chances for success will certainly increase.

Note the careful consideration of the type of advisor they chose. Each time Tony and Jay put a new business deal together, they seek the advice of an attorney/CPA with experience and expertise. Like David Hammer, Tony's CPA is also an entrepreneur; in fact, he has made 80 percent of his wealth in venture deals. Because of their background, both men realize that their job is to help their clients make deals happen, not to kill them. Although they point out the risks involved, they focus on how to deal with risk and minimize it rather than avoiding it. The same goes for corporate leaders; you should find advisors who will look for ways to help you and your organization succeed, within reasonable risks – not just give you all the reasons why something won't work.

Now let's look more in depth at the four-step process.

Step 1: Identify your issues and opportunities

When you sit down with an advisor, you need to know what advice you want. There are many tools you can use to identify your issues and opportunities. Sometimes it's as simple as spending time in self-reflection, thinking about what you need. It's also a great idea to brainstorm with your team, or you may recognize an issue from something someone says during a phone call or a meeting. Often, however, you need to use strategic tools to apply a laser focus on your real issues and opportunities.

The SWOT analysis is a great tool that has been around a long time. By identifying your strengths, weaknesses, opportunities, and threats, you can achieve clarity on where you want to be versus where you are currently. An advisor (one or more) can help you focus on the main things you need to do in order to close that gap.

We've included a SWOT template (below) to help you document your:

1. Strengths (what you and/or your organization do well; the top qualities you can leverage)
2. Weaknesses (areas to improve or change)
3. Opportunities (external positive dynamics you and/or your business can profit from)
4. Threats (reasons why you might fail)

SWOT Analysis

1. Strengths:	
2. Weaknesses:	
3. Opportunities:	
4. Threats:	

The MOLO (More of, Less of) exercise is another excellent tool. It identifies the things you do that produce the greatest impact (the things you need to do more of), as well as those things that may actually be reducing your overall effectiveness (things you need to do less of).

By completing the MOLO Matrix below, you will discover:

1. What is working well and what is not as you pursue your vision
2. What you need to change to be more effective
3. The High Leverage Activities that deserve the majority of your time and effort.

MOLO Matrix

What Do I Need to...	Actions	Why
...Do More Of?		
...Do Less Of?		
...Start Doing?		
...Stop Doing?		
...Start Doing Differently?		

In Tony's 2009 book, *Strategic Acceleration: Succeed at the Speed of Life*, he introduced the concept of High Leverage Activities (HLAs). HLAs are those activities that you should be doing most of the time to move you closer to your vision. Over the years since he introduced the concept, Tony's top level clients have found HLAs to be the single most powerful principle in maximizing leverage, because they prioritize action according to which actions are high leverage (produce superior results faster) and which actions are low leverage. HLAs are the secret to utilizing minimal resources to achieve maximum results.

Assessments that measure and evaluate your strengths and weaknesses are another great tool for determining your issues and opportunities, including where you stand in relation to your goals. Whether you use the 360 assessment tool or any of the many excellent online assessments, you will often discover a bigger picture of where you are and where you could be. (Visit www.tonyjeary.com for many powerful free assessments.)

As you're endeavoring to identify your issues and opportunities, keep in mind that we all have *Blind Spots*. *Blind Spots* are "mental scotomas" – blockages in your psychological awareness, or areas where you lack insight. In other words, *Blind Spots* are things on your *Belief Window* that you can't see unless uncovered by something or someone else. In order to move through life better, you need to get advice that will help you uncover your *Blind Spots* and change your *Belief Window*.

Jay was once asked to mentor a man who had a pretty substantial business and was, in fact, a leader in his industry. Jay's style as a mentor includes asking hard questions, because he believes you can't help someone if you can't get all the facts. As he tried to work with this entrepreneur to see what his challenges were and where he needed help, he asked some very hard personal and financial questions; but the man kept skirting them. Jay finally realized that this mentee had a blind spot: He believed the best way to do business was to hold his cards close to his vest and not share personal and financial information with anyone. After Jay pointed out his blind spot and told him he couldn't help him if he didn't open up, the mentee thought about it a while and said, "Well, I guess if you go to the doctor, you have to expect to take your pants down." He modified his *Belief Window* and starting answering Jay's questions, and Jay was able to give him the help he needed.

A blind spot can often be a shortcoming in the way you're thinking about a particular issue. For example, maybe you have a blind spot about firing someone, because you've never come to the conclusion that it truly benefits everyone involved. The company is better off; the other employees are better off; and the person you're going to fire, who is obviously not the right fit for the job, will be better off relocating to another company where he or she will be happier. Whatever your *Blind Spots* are, they are probably keeping you from being the best you can be. We can't emphasize enough the importance of finding the right advisors who will help you uncover your *Blind Spots*.

Step 2: Determine the best resource(s) to go after to get your advice from

Once you determine what your issues and opportunities are, you need to get some insight as to where to go from there. Your issue could be raising capital; it could be selling your company, or a merger or an acquisition; it could be that you need a partnership agreement; or it could be that you need to structure your compensation package for a new position. Whatever it is, you need to get the best advice you can to help you make a decision.

Let's say the issue you've identified is that you need to fire someone, as we mentioned above. You know it needs to be done, but you don't know the best way to go about it. You need to ask yourself, "Who do I have in my advisory pool that has the experience, expertise, knowledge, and tools to help me? Should I go to one advisor, or would a combination of people be better?" You may have a mentor who knows how to help you, or your coach may be the best one to go to. Or you may possibly need to get legal advice. Trusted colleagues may have an opinion; but unless they have the level of knowledge and experience you need, be careful to recognize their opinions for what they are. There may be some great books, articles, videos, or URLs available to help you, as well. Keep in mind, though, that there could be special circumstances that may need to be discussed in person with an advisor.

Step 3: Gather options or possible solutions, and then review the plusses and minuses (including the risks)

After careful consideration of all the advisors available to you, let's say you decide that your coach is the best one to give you counsel on this particular issue. A master coach might say something like, "I've helped a lot of top executives and entrepreneurs fire people when it becomes necessary, and I've developed a list of six things that will help you fire someone well. Let's talk about them and see how they can apply to your particular situation." You may have also found some information on the Internet you want to include in the discussion, and one or two of your trusted colleagues may have jumped in with some ideas. It's important to put everything on the table in your discussion with your coach so he can come up with some concrete options for you to consider.

We've talked about the advantages of having longevity with your advisors; but we need to point out here that there will probably be some situations where you may need an advisor for a specific situation, and you will only use that advisor one time for that purpose. For example, Jay had helped a friend work through some issues with the help of a patent attorney a few years ago, and the friend ended up spending a couple of million dollars with the attorney in the course of two or three patent suits. In the process of helping his friend, Jay got acquainted with the patent attorney, who happened to be one of the best in the nation. Later, Jay had a challenge with a patent issue at his GPS Tracking Company. He called the attorney, and he worked with Jay to resolve the issue. (Incidentally, since Jay's friend had spent so much with the attorney, and since the attorney understood that the tracking company was a startup, he sent Jay a very friendly bill for his services) Hopefully, Jay will not need his advice again, although he will certainly refer him to anyone who has a patent issue.

Step 4: Take action accordingly

After you weigh all the options from all sources of advice, you have to take action. You can be really clear on what your issues and opportunities are, and you can strategize with an advisor and get really focused on what you need to do to resolve your issues; but without action you're not going to get results.

One of the biggest mistakes people make is that they wait to get 100 percent of the facts before they take action. It's better to start executing with a calculated risk because you're not 100 percent knowledgeable than it is to wait for days or weeks or months in order to get all of the facts. Some people spend all their time researching and forget to take action. We call that analysis paralysis. Preparation and planning are important, but excessive preparation is nothing more than procrastination.

In Tony's book *Strategic Acceleration*, he pointed out that there are two basic types of procrastination – one is negative and one is positive. Positive procrastination is simply taking a calculated pause in order to get good insight and/or reflect and gather your thoughts. Often, though, people continually find excuses for putting things off: I don't have time, I don't have enough information, I can do it tomorrow, someone else can do it better, etc. That's called negative procrastination, and it leads to negative results. In fact, nothing restricts results and effectiveness more than negative procrastination.

Tony's solution to negative procrastination is something he calls *Production Before Perfection (PBP)* – getting started with whatever you have and perfecting as you go. In other words, act first and get it perfect later. You can't get results until you do something; if you do nothing, that's exactly what you will get. If you get started, though, you'll pick up momentum that will head you toward the results you want.

Go as far as you can see with what you have, and then you will see farther. You don't always have to have everything you need or understand all the details in the beginning. Get started and resist the temptation to procrastinate. *Production Before Perfection* (PBP) is a catalyst for outstanding results.

V.I.P.s

- There are four simple steps to help you navigate through the choices and options available for getting advice:

  - Identify your issues and opportunities

  - Determine the best resource(s) to go after to get your advice from

  - Gather options or possible solutions from your advisor(s), and then review the plusses and minuses (including the risks)

  - Take action accordingly

- Use these effective tools to strategically identify your issues and opportunities:

  - A SWOT Analysis, which will help you identify your strengths, weaknesses, opportunities, and threats

  - The MOLO (More of, Less of) exercise, which identifies the things you do that produce the greatest impact (what you need to do more of), as well as those that may actually be reducing your overall effectiveness (what you need to do less of)

  - HLAs (activities you should be doing most of the time to move you closer to your vision), which prioritize action according to which actions are high leverage (produce superior results faster) and which actions are low leverage

  - Assessments that measure and evaluate your strengths and weaknesses, including where you stand in relation to your goals.

- Positive procrastination is simply taking a calculated pause in order to get good insight and/or reflect and gather your thoughts.

- Negative procrastination is continually finding excuses for putting things off; nothing restricts results and effectiveness more than negative procrastination.

- *Production Before Perfection (PBP)*, getting started with whatever you have and perfecting as you go, is a catalyst for outstanding results.

Section III: Making It Work

CHAPTER 5

ROLES AND RELATIONSHIPS

Tony had coached the executive team of a trucking company for six years. One day the company's former president, who knew Tony well, called him and said, "I have the opportunity to become the president of one of two trucking companies, and I need you to help me think through which job I should accept." So Tony worked with him to analyze all of the pieces and determine which company was best for him. The client accepted the offer from USA Truck (the company we mentioned in Chapter 2), and four days after the president took the helm he flew his executive team to Tony's studio so he could help them build a plan to take the company where they wanted to go. It was a public company that was losing $10 million a year, and he had to turn it around quickly. At that time, the stock was at $4 a share. For the next 24 months straight, because of the trust and history the president had with Tony, he brought his team into Tony's studio every 90 days – like clockwork, quarter after quarter. Within that 24-month period the stock went from $4 a share to over $30 a share – more than a 700 percent increase.

TRUST AND LONGEVITY

Tony's longevity as the coach for the previous company and the results he had helped that company achieve had allowed him to establish an excellent level of trust and rapport with this client. Trust is a significant factor in any advisory relationship; it's far better to work with people with whom you've already built up a trust factor, if possible. If you're just beginning a relationship with a mentor, coach, or paid advisor you don't know, hopefully you've used the selection criteria in your search that we've talked about in this book and have determined in advance that their track record of results merits your trust in working with them. It's just plain smart to pick people with an outstanding track record; and once you find the right advisors, it's best to stick with them. Longevity provides a definite gain in efficiency and multiplies your ability to achieve Mastery.

Because of his history with Tony and the high level of trust he had established with him in his previous position, this company president was confident that Tony and his team could help him make good things happen in his new position. With Tony's help, he placed his bet on the right company; then he immediately brought his people under Tony's coaching so he could help them turn the company around. Members of the executive team told Tony later that the first time they went to his studio, they were thinking, "What are we doing here in someone's back yard?" Two years later, they and the shareholders were singing Tony's praises and darned happy they engaged the president to do his magic.

If you invest the energy into hiring any type of advisor, you want to think about the additional value that person could provide to you in the next month, the next year, or five or ten years down the road. Jay and Tony both have attorneys from whom they've been seeking advice for approximately three decades. They recommend that during the interview/discovery stage you consider your vision of how that relationship could play out in the future. If the relationship is a good match, your visions should be in alignment.

LANGUAGE

One of the benefits of longevity is that, once you've worked together for a while, you will develop a distinctive language between you that will allow you to shortcut thoughts and ideas. At some point, a look, a gesture, or a phrase will communicate a complete thought without the need for lengthy discussion. After a while, you may find that you can finish each other's sentences, "read' what the other is thinking before a word is spoken, or realize a need before it is verbalized. That's often the way Tony and Jay connect with each other. As they communicate back and forth, they can read each other so well that Jay, as Tony's mentor, can sometimes say just a few words and Tony says, "I get it."

In our example, Tony and the president of USA Truck quickly developed such a unique language between them that they could text or email short phrases to each other with full understanding of what the other was saying. Often, late at night before the president was to make board calls or have an all-hands-on-deck meeting with his people the next morning, Tony would just send two- or three-word messages to remind him of important things to remember – like "Appreciate your team." Because of their history and all the times they had talked about that topic, those three words were enough to remind him to effectively weave appreciation into his speech.

The longevity and trust factor both Jay and Tony enjoy with many of their advisors allows them to easily route things to them when a need arises. Then, because of that history, their advisors can often quickly shorthand back to them the distinctions they need in a way they can best understand, which helps them evaluate their options and make decisions. That ability has a multiplying impact on Mastery. If you consistently rotate to new advisors, you just don't get the same win as you have with longevity. Strong leaders look for ways to not only surround themselves with advisors, but also to keep those advisors around them for a long time.

COMMUNICATION STRUCTURE

One of the first things you need to do when you find the right advisor(s) is determine the best way to communicate, whether that's by phone, by email, or in person.

Generally speaking, when you're using mentors, you need to yield to their wishes. They are giving up valuable time to pour into your life – for free – and you need to accommodate their wishes as much as possible or practical. Jay prefers face-to-face meetings with his mentees, and phone calls over email or texting. (In Jay's words, "Members of the older generation, like myself, usually prefer the telephone when face-to-face isn't practical; we realize it's primitive, but it's still highly effective.") He chooses to have Tony come to his office for their mentoring sessions, usually on Sunday afternoon. Tony is happy to oblige because of the value he places on Jay's advice.

With a coach or other paid advisors, you have more latitude and can choose the communication style. Tony asks his clients how they prefer to communicate with him, as their coach. The client in our example, the president of USA Truck, preferred a combination of all types of communication – the gamut, from texting to email, to phone, and in person.

When Tony is coaching people, his goal is to structure the communication in a way that will serve them best, and that always involves saving time. He has developed a unique system that will not only accomplish that, but it will also give them back much of the time they're investing in his coaching. Understanding the importance of making every minute count for the CEOs and executives he works with, he tells them, "When I'm coaching you, you don't even have to take your own notes. Because I work with people like you who have such high capital at stake and who need to make such premium use of your time, I have set up a system where someone is always in the room or on the line taking notes when we're talking. That way, whether we're in my studio or you're driving while we're talking, you can be assured that we're capturing the points and actions we discuss. Then after the session or call, we will immediately email to you the list of actions we agreed on; and if you prefer, we can send you all the detailed notes, as well. You don't have to worry about writing anything down." Tony even takes it one step further. He tells the client, "You don't even have to develop your own agenda. During our coaching sessions, I will hear what you want; and before the next call or meeting I will send an agenda for you to preapprove, so we'll be ready to jump right in and get started when the time comes. Now, do you want to have our session on the phone, in person, or by email?" His clients love it. Sometimes they ask his team to email the notes to their assistants, or they may say, "Would you email my Director of Marketing on this?" Suddenly Tony and his team have upped the bar in the value they provide, because the communication structure has not only saved the client's time, but it has also helped cascade important information to his or her staff. It's that kind of innovation that separates Tony out as a Master coach. Look for a coach that has a hand-picked team like Tony's that allows him or her to make life easier for clients in the ways described above. Every action is designed to give the utmost benefit and value to the client.

Tony is extremely sensitive to the way he communicates with his clients. He has an arsenal of tools that is second to none. Yet he knows his clients are not interested in everything he has gathered over his 30 years of advising;

they only want that one little kernel that will make a financial difference to them right then. He tells them, "Guess what! You have access to all of it; and you don't even need to know what's there. When you tell me what you need, I'll think about what I have that will help you. And if I tell you something or give you something you don't want, you can say, 'That doesn't fit me.' I won't argue with you. I'm serving up things for you. You decide."

A mentor is a little bit different. A mentor may say, "Look, I've been where you want to go and I've been very successful in the process. You need to really listen to me." Again, you don't want to let your mentor (or any other advisor) make your decisions for you, but you do need to listen respectfully and seriously consider the advice he or she is pouring into you to see if it fits your situation. Jay tells his mentees', "I can give you the absolutely best course of action to pursue in a given situation; but if it doesn't fit your personality or feel comfortable to you, don't do it."

For trusted colleagues, you can work out a communication structure that is beneficial to all. When Tony's working on a book cover, he may have six or seven choices that he sends to them by email and says, "Please vote," without having to go into a long explanation. They know he writes a lot of books, and they can just send short emails back, saying something like, "I like No. 3 or No. 4." They don't have to call him and ask a lot of questions. If they happen to have a good idea for another option, they may send him a picture and say, "Here's an idea; but other than that, I vote for No. 3." Minimal words, maximum input.

Texting provides a little more privacy than email. Email, though, affords more diplomacy; and it can be forwarded, giving you multiplying positive impacts for well thought-out messages. Those are things to consider when you're discussing communication choices with your advisor(s), along with time efficiency, how the messages can be saved for the future, and how they can be cataloged and reused. Sometimes a recorded phone call is good, and sometimes a web call is better so you can show things in real time.

There are times when the appropriate communication structure may involve flying across the country to meet with someone face-to-face. As we mentioned in the introduction, Tony and Jay did just that within weeks of their first meeting, to meet with one of Jay's trusted colleagues who gave

Tony invaluable advice. In another example, Tony was coaching the president of HP Canada when he accepted the position of president with another company in North America. Again, because of the trust, the history, and the success that he had previously established with Tony, this president asked him to fly to New York within a couple of days of his taking the position. They sat down together and penciled out a strategy for his new position, and the clarity he achieved in that one three-hour face-to-face session allowed him to really make magic in the first one hundred days of his first year as president of the new company. He already had a history of extraordinary success using Tony's Strategic Acceleration methodology (clarity, focus, and execution); and, because he knew it worked, he was now ready to integrate it into the culture of his new company.

TOOLS

When possible, choose advisors who use models you can apply (in a way you can use them) so you end up with a language, tools, and processes that match your style of preference. For example, Tony and his team meet with his CPA in October of each year; and they develop a spreadsheet that links all of his financials together into one master, which ends up formulating a preliminary set of tax returns. Because this tool allows Tony to see where he's headed, tax wise, for the year, he can make adjustments as needed to optimize his finances. They make a list of things Tony needs to do for the next two or three months to complete that year. That's a very valuable tool that works well for Tony, and one he would hate to do without.

(Notice that his CPA communicates with Tony in the way he prefers. The CPA comes to his studio for an all-day meeting with Tony's business manager, and they work out all of the details. Tony doesn't have to gather his team and all of their files together and spend hours in his CPA's office. All he has to do is walk in during the last hour of the meeting in his studio and work through with his CPA and business manager the list of decisions he needs to make and actions he needs to take before the end of the year. It's the perfect communication structure for Tony.)

Some advisors bring their tools with them, and some you can customize with your advisors as you go. As we've mentioned, Tony has a whole arsenal of tools that he shares with his clients, choosing those that are applicable to the particular person he's working with. He maintains this giant tool box so he can provide value in the least amount of time, based on all of his experiences.

When Tony is working with a new client, he frequently starts with a tool Tony has coined as a *Stakeholder Matrix*. He has his clients identify all the stakeholders involved – including the shareholders, the board, the chairman, the president, strategic partners, customers, clients, associates, and members. By identifying all the stakeholders, what they all want from the success of that particular business, and what they're willing to do to make it succeed, the clarity – for both Tony and the client - goes sky high on how everyone fits together. Tony has a better picture, which enhances the whole playing field of the relationship; and the client has far greater clarity on what his or her needs are. This tool, which can often be deployed in less than an hour, helps his clients ensure that all the stakeholders are winning.

DEFINING THE RELATIONSHIP

After choosing your advisors, it's important to look at the roles you each will play and define the relationship. Keep in mind that advisors, because of their experience in their own areas of expertise, frequently have the ability to look at your situation from a totally different mindset and viewpoint than you have the background to do – and that's one of their huge values.

When Jay was taking flying lessons, he and another student, John, would usually schedule their lessons together; one would observe and learn from the back seat while the other had his lesson, and then they would switch places. One day his friend wasn't able to make it, so Jay went up for his lesson alone with his instructor. They went around the patch two or three times and landed, and the instructor told Jay to pull over. He said, "Jay, I'm getting out. You're going to solo today." Jay was totally shocked and said, "How in the world can you say I'm going to solo? John, as we both know, makes a perfect landing every time he lands, and he hasn't soloed yet. I have messed up almost every landing I have ever made, and you're telling me I'm supposed to solo ahead of John?" With all of the wisdom of a Master advisor, the instructor said, "Jay, you have messed up so many landings that I am totally comfortable with your ability to recover from a bad landing. I have no idea what John is going to do when he messes one up."

What Jay had on his *Belief Window* was totally different than what the instructor had on his. Our advisors have been where we want to go much more than we have, which qualifies them to give us insight. In his experience with working with people over the years, the instructor had learned a lot more than Jay had in his short time of training to be a pilot. The roles were clear: the instructor had the history, expertise, and success to qualify him as a Master advisor; Jay, as the advisee, who was there to soak up as much of the instructor's knowledge as he could.

When you find an advisor who is a great match for you, it's essential that you define the relationship on paper. The absence of a formal agreement can lessen the value of the relationship, because there is no solid roadmap to follow that will lead to ultimate value and superior results. The agreement, *at minimum*, should include these pieces:

1. The advisee's situation, including the issues and the need
2. The goal of the relationship and the expected outcome
3. The process you will use to measure the outcomes
4. The frequency, times, and locations of the meetings
5. What each person should bring to each meeting
6. The extent of the relationship (one-time, for a defined period of time, or ongoing)

Entrepreneurs' Organization (EO), is a global peer-to-peer network exclusively for entrepreneurs. Biz Owners Ed has provided many mentors for EO's Dallas chapter. Founded in 1987 to help leading business owners on their path to greater professional success and personal fulfillment, EO is a global community that enriches members' lives through dynamic peer-to-peer learning, once-in-a-lifetime experiences, and connections to experts (www.eonetwork.org). To become a member of EO, an entrepreneur must be the owner, founder, or majority stakeholder of a company with at least $1 million in annual revenue. The EO mentor/mentee agreement, a 30-page document, contains these elements:

1. A code of conduct, in which both parties agree to the standards of honesty, openness, and integrity.

2. The goals for the mentorship, to be completed by the mentee with input from the mentor. It includes ways the mentor can best provide encouragement, corrective feedback, and help with the mentee's business and/or personal issues.

3. A planning tool for the first meeting, in which the mentee and/or mentor provide:
   - Background information
   - Dates for the three-month introductory period
   - The mentee's needs in the areas of knowledge, skills, attitude changes, and resources
   - The mentee's greatest challenges
   - Assistance the mentor can/would like to provide
   - Other individuals/resources that may be helpful
   - Limits or constraints in the partnership
   - Preferences for communication/feedback
   - How success of the mentorship will be measured
   - Best times/places to meet
   - Date, time, and place of next meeting
   - Actions needed before the next meeting

4. A planning tool for regular meetings, which includes:
   - Progress made/successes to celebrate
   - Challenges
   - Specific goals/topics for that meeting
   - Key learnings from that meeting
   - Follow-up actions for mentee, and for mentor, if applicable
   - Next meeting date, location, and tentative topics

5. The EO Mentee/Mentor Guide, which includes:
   - Best practices for a successful mentor/mentee relationship
   - Mindset and behaviors (core behaviors and beliefs on mentorship)
   - Smart goals (effective goal-setting techniques)

- Tools and resources for holding productive meetings
- Strategies for making the relationship work (strengthening the relationship and maintaining momentum)
- Preparation and transition guide for finishing strong
- Troubleshooting guide that addresses mentor and mentee challenges

Although this is an excellent agreement and it contains a lot of helpful information for both the advisor and the advisee, you don't always have to go into such great detail. We do recommend, though, that you define as accurately as possible the roles, the relationship, the expected outcomes, and the process you will use to measure the outcomes.

V.I.P.s

- Trust is a significant factor in any advisory relationship; it's far better to work with people with whom you've already built up a trust factor, if possible.

- Longevity provides a definite gain in efficiency and multiplies your ability to achieve Mastery.

- During the interview stage, consider your vision of how that relationship could play out in the future. If the relationship is a good match, your visions should be in alignment.

- One of the benefits of longevity is that, once you've worked together for a while, you will develop a distinctive language between you that will allow you to shortcut thoughts and ideas.

- When you find the right advisor(s), determine the best way to communicate.

- When possible, choose advisors who use a model you can apply (in a way you can use it) so you end up with a language, tools, and processes that match your style of preference.

- After choosing your advisors, look at the roles you each will play and define the relationship on paper. The absence of a formal agreement lessens the value of the relationship, because there is no roadmap to follow that will lead to ultimate value and superior results.

CHAPTER 6

SESSIONS: OBJECTIVES, AGENDAS, AND FOLLOW-UP

"After you've decided what you want, you have to believe it's possible, and possible for you, not just for other people. Then you need to seek out models, mentors, and coaches."

– JACK CANFIELD

It had not taken too many meetings with his mentee for Jay to figure out the problem. The mentee had a specific area of Mastery, and he really excelled as a consultant in that arena. But because he enjoyed consulting on other topics in which he was not nearly as qualified, he kept drifting away from his area of Mastery, even though he had to rely on the expertise of others on those issues.

Jay spent considerable time preparing for their next meeting. He suggested to the mentee that, before their next session, he make four lists: one list of his qualifications as a consultant for his primary area of expertise, and one list of his qualifications in each of the other three areas in which he had been dabbling.

The first thing they did at their next meeting was to review the mentee's four lists. Though it was clear that he offered less than Mastery in all but his primary area of expertise, the mentee was still not convinced that he should abandon the three secondary areas he enjoyed. At that point, Jay asked him to read the following:

> Bald-headed men, for example, are bald for no other reason than their fear of criticism. Heads become bald because of the tight fitting bands of hats which cut off the circulation from the roots of the hair. Men wear hats, not because they actually need them, but mainly because "everyone is doing it." The individual falls into

line and does likewise, lest some other individual CRITICISE him. Women seldom have bald heads, or even thin hair, because they wear hats which fit their heads loosely, the only purpose of the hats being adornment.

When the mentee finished, Jay asked him how he would rate the author as an expert on baldness. The mentee answered that, on a scale of 1-10, the writer would be at or below 0. At that point, Jay disclosed that those words had been written by Napoleon Hill and were in one of the world's greatest books on building wealth, *Think and Grow Rich*. Napoleon Hill got away with straying briefly from his area of expertise only because the book was otherwise a true masterpiece.

Jay had finally made his point. The mentee refocused on his one area of Mastery and went on to excel in that area of his expertise.

As you can see from this story, a lot of preparation goes into each session with an advisor, and sometimes the outcome can mean life or death for a person's business or career. If Jay's mentee had continued on his current course, his results would have been mediocre at best. As his mentor, Jay had a clear objective: to figure out how to keep him from sabotaging his own career. At the same time, his mentee had to come to the sessions prepared and with an open mind. It may have taken some time to convince the mentee that he needed to make some major changes, but in the end he was open to Jay's suggestions.

THE PROCESS: OBJECTIVES AND AGENDAS

When advisors and advisees are working together, there is a process involved. You may remember that when Tony and Jay met for the first time as mentor/mentee, Jay lowered his conference table from the ceiling and they both pulled out their legal pads with their objectives and an agenda they had brought to the meeting. They knew right away they would hit it off, because they were both into objectives and agendas. Not surprisingly, because they were both professionals who had been advisors for many years, their agendas flowed together very well. Over the years, they have perfected their process. Now, when Tony goes to meet with Jay, he brings a list of five or six – and perhaps even ten – topics that he wants to seek Jay's advice on. Tony respects Jay's time; he understands that if Jay is going to take his valuable time to meet with him, they need to have objectives laid out in an organized agenda so they can stay on track. Normally he will email those objectives and the agenda to Jay a few days ahead of their meeting, which gives him a chance to review them thoroughly on his own time and put some thought into them, rather than having to speak off the top of his head when something is thrown at him spontaneously. This allows Jay to pour more wisdom and insight into Tony when they meet together and really increases the impact Jay can have.

Of the more than 40 books Tony has written, 26 of them have been on presentations; and three of those 26 are about how to have great meetings. All three books emphasize the importance of having clear objectives and a well organized agenda before you go into any type of meeting. Jay likes it when Tony comes to him and says with clarity, "Here are my issues, here are my objectives, and here's the agenda." Sometimes Tony brings a file with copies of articles, graphics, or other documents related to his objectives, and sometimes he emails those items to Jay in advance, along with the agenda.

When Tony is coaching someone, either in person or on the phone, and that person says, "Here are the three things I want to talk about," it immediately escalates the effectiveness of their meeting. Sometimes Tony will present a suggested agenda, and the client will come back and say, "No, I want to talk about these two things." When that happens, Tony says, "No problem. Let's scrap my agenda and go with these two things." He understands that the client must have had some issues come up that require top priority.

When you have a scheduled meeting with an advisor, the best option is to email your objectives and agenda to your advisor a few days ahead of the meeting. There are times, though, when it's appropriate to present your objectives more informally, such as at the beginning of a call or an impromptu meeting with your advisor. For example, Tony may call Jay and say, "I really need to get your thoughts on a couple of issues, and here's what they are. I need to make a decision this afternoon. Can you help me?" The objectives are not written down, but he clearly presents them at the beginning of the call. The idea is that, as a standard protocol, both you and your advisor must have clarity on what you want to accomplish in the meeting or phone call.

You can be as formal or informal as you want with your objectives. You can type them on the computer; or you can write them on a flip chart, on a legal pad, or even on the back of an envelope – however you want to do it. The point is, just get them down on paper and then check them off as you go through your agenda. When you're meeting with someone to get advice, it helps to have your thoughts together. When Tony's on the phone with his coach, for example, and he has three things he wants to go over with him, he has his objectives written on his legal pad and he or his team is taking notes as they talk. At the same time, though, he's checking things off his list of objectives as they cover them.

When Tony meets with his CPA or his attorney, he will often go over to the flipchart and outline the objectives of their meeting. Or sometimes he will email the objectives to them ahead of time, especially if there are things they need to prepare in advance or bring with them. Since he pays those advisors a high-dollar figure by the hour, clarifying the objectives up front helps them stay on track and move through the agenda more quickly. For example, he may say to his CPA in their annual meeting in October, "These are the three things we need to do today. We're going to make our plan for the next 60 days to close out the year, we're going to look at the tax position to see how it's going to look for this year, and then we're going to make a list of the actions we need to take."

When you're meeting with any advisor you pay by the hour, it only makes sense to drive the meeting with your own objectives and agenda. If you go into the meeting unprepared and allow the paid advisor to drive the agenda, you're risking the efficiency and outcome of the meeting.

This principle is important no matter where you're seeking advice. When Tony sends an email to a trusted colleague, for example, he may say, "I'd like for you to vote on my book cover." It's simple and direct. "Just pick one and tell me why you chose it." When you're evaluating yourself and re-flecting on your successes and mistakes, your objective is not to beat your-self up for your mistakes and tear down your self-esteem. Your objective is to pull out kernels that you can learn from, make adjustments, and go forward wiser than you were before.

It's even important to have objectives when you start to read a book. Tony will often start to read a book with the purpose of gleaning kernels that will help him in his life, and then realize that there's an easier way to get to the bottom line. For example, if the book presents eight principles that will help him in a certain area, he can go to the Internet and search for the book online to get those eight principles. He doesn't need to burn up any more hours reading the book, because he found another route to accomplish his objective of getting the eight principles that the author spent 20 years learning. Of course, he can still read the book for enjoyment if that is his objective.

Sometimes Tony will give added value to his clients by telling them about a book he thinks they should read, and then sending them the book summary he or his staff has created so they can preview the book. That way, they can decide, based on their own objectives, whether to spend several hours reading the book or just glean what they need from the summary.

One thing to remember is that your objectives should trump your agenda. Here's what we mean by that: When you go into a meeting with your advisor(s), you should have a set of objectives you want to accomplish and an agenda that you think is going to achieve the objectives. But you want to be flexible enough to change the agenda, if need be, to make sure all of your objectives are met. Be prepared for things that could happen – like a phone call that requires your or your advisor's attention or getting bogged down in a discussion and letting the time run out. You need to be fluid enough to zero in on the most urgent objectives first and move the others to the end of the agenda. In other words, you may need to rearrange the priorities in keeping with the priority objectives.

Another thing to remember when you're meeting with your mentor, coach, or other paid advisor, is to be sure and include on the agenda a start and stop time. Tony and Jay normally meet for an hour and a half, or two hours if they have some flex time. It's just a good idea to have that efficiency built into your structure so you can keep things moving within the time frame.

Follow-Up

Follow-up is one of the most important aspects of an advisor/advisee relationship, and many people miss the simplicity and impact of an email follow-up. A good follow-up email will document the main points of the discussion and list any actions recommended by the advisor, as understood by the advisee. This gives the advisor an opportunity to confirm the advisee's understanding and/or clarify any misunderstandings.

Within a couple of hours after Jay and Tony meet, Tony sends a follow-up email to Jay. He thanks Jay for his time and input; and then he lists all the main points and the actions that Jay, as his mentor, recommended. Tony may say, "This is what I heard and these are the seven action items you suggested." Jay may come back with, "Yes, you got six of them right, but you didn't get what I was saying on that last one," and then he will clarify what he said. Jay appreciates the fact that Tony takes the time to document their discussion and follow up with him. It shows Jay that Tony values his input and that he has clarity on the points they discussed.

Whether Tony acts on that input or not is up to Tony. Out of those seven things, for example, Tony may think three are a fit for him and four are not. That's fine with Jay, because he realizes that Tony is a better judge of what fits in his situation and what doesn't. Jay understands the role of an advisor – to give advice to the advisee, not to make decisions for him or her.

Before his next meeting with Jay, Tony may follow up with another email that says, "These are the action steps I've taken." Notice that he *doesn't* hold up a flag and say, "I liked these three, but I didn't think the other four were a fit." He highlights only the applicable points and focuses on the positive, rather than on the things he chooses not to pursue. You don't ever want to insult a mentor who is pouring into you. What you want to do is show your mentors (and other advisors) how much you appreciate them, and you can do that by reporting back and reinforcing the value of their input.

You may remember that Tony often does the follow-up for the executives he coaches by having a member of his team on the call or in the room during the session who is taking notes and documenting the conversation. The executive can be in his airplane, driving his car, or anywhere else, and he doesn't have to do anything but take part in the discussion. Immediately after the session, Tony's team trims the notes and sends the actions they agreed on to the executive and his or her assistant, plus more details if that's what the executive wants. That follow-up system is a huge bonus for his clients.

Tony has decades of VIP notes from his meetings with his own coaches and mentors. Each time they meet, he sends a follow-up email that says, "This is my biggest takeaway from our meeting." It takes self-discipline to do the follow-up. Often, you're the one who benefits from the follow-up more than your advisor. You want to have a system that ensures you're following through on the good advice you received. It's a tool to hold yourself accountable, and it also serves as a clarification tool to ensure that you're both on the same page. If you only got 80 percent of the points right and missed one or two of the most important kernels, your advisor may come back and say, "Yes, but you missed what I was saying. The main thing is this."

You can even enhance the advice you glean from a book by doing what Tony does. He decided a long time ago that he would highlight and summarize the books he reads, so he could have a permanent reminder of the important points of the book. He puts those book summaries in his arsenal to share with his clients as an added value, so they can benefit from his follow-up, as well.

There is substantial value in the follow-up. Advisors enjoy working with people who take action and then report back what action they've taken. Follow-up needs to be a big part of the advisor/advisee relationship, whether it's with a mentor, a coach, another paid professional advisor, or even a book.

V.I.P.s

- When advisors and advisees are working together, there is a process involved; it starts with clear objectives and a well organized agenda to help them stay on track.

- As a standard protocol, both you and your advisor must have clarity on what you want to accomplish in the meeting or phone call.

- Your objectives should trump your agenda; be flexible enough to change the agenda, if need be, to make sure all of your objectives are met.

- Follow-up is one of the most important aspects of an advisor/advisee relationship. A good follow-up email will document the main points of the discussion and list any actions recommended by the advisor, as understood by the advisee.

- In the follow-up email, highlight only the applicable points and focus on the positive, rather than on the things you choose not to pursue.

- You want to show your advisors how much you appreciate them, and you can do that by reporting back and reinforcing the value of their input. Advisors enjoy working with people who take action and then report back what action they've taken.

CHAPTER 7

YOUR ADVISORS' CONNECTIONS CAN BECOME A *FORCE MULTIPLIER* FOR YOU

"Leaders understand the ultimate power of relationships."
—TOM PETERS

A member of the Mitsubishi executive team called Tony about five years ago and said, "We would like to hire you to make a presentation over a period of three days at our distributor conference in Hawaii." He said, "We want you to talk about Clarity on the first day, Focus on the second, and Execution on the third."

"Great!" Tony said. "While I'm there, don't you want me to do more than that?"

"No," the executive replied. "All we want you to do is speak."

Tony said, "No, you really want me to come and do much more than give a speech. I've worked with other Japanese companies over the years, like Sony, Hitachi, and Firestone; and since I understand Japanese clients, and I understand distributor meetings, I can do a lot more while I'm there. If you'll arrange for me to play golf during the afternoon sessions with the top distributors, I'll impact them, as well. And I can do extra sessions during lunches and attend special dinners with select distributors at night while I'm there."

Excited to hear of Tony's expertise and experience, the executive agreed that he should do all of these other things while he was there. "How much is all of this going to cost?" he asked.

"About $80,000," Tony replied.

"Wow! We knew you were going to be expensive," the executive said.

"$80,000 is a small fee for all the impact I'm going to have," Tony replied.

"What can you do for half of that?" the executive went on to ask.

"I'll do it all for half."

"You will?"

"If I blow you away, though," Tony said, "then go find some more budget."

"It's a deal," the executive replied.

After the conference was over, the executive came to Tony and said, "You really did blow us away, and we found another $125,000. We want you to come and put your magic into our organization." Thus, Tony's relationship with Mitsubishi went from just speaking at one event to his advising its entire executive team on an ongoing basis (for five years, at the time of this publishing).

Six months later, though, he entrenched his value to the Mitsubishi team even more. He was in a meeting with the executive team one day, and they were about to make a commitment for $500,000 for a PR and marketing campaign. Tony made one phone call during that meeting to someone in his Rolodex; and with that one call, he was able to connect them with a person who could do for around $20,000 what they were about to spend $300,000 of the $500,000 for – a savings of $280,000. Now, that's a force multiplier!

Because of that one Rolodex connection and the value Tony consistently provides as their coach, his relationship with the Mitsubishi executive team is still ongoing. When you're bringing advisors into your world, whether they are mentors, coaches, or paid advisors, you really want them to bring their Rolodex into the relationship, as well. As you are doing your due diligence research and the initial interview, it's important to find out how well connected they are and how open-minded they are to bringing their people to you. If you're working with a doctor, for example, you might say, "Can you tell me about the team of doctors you work with?" If you're interviewing a CPA, you could say, "Would you tell me about the team of advisors you work with?" Whoever the advisor may be, work questions similar to these into the interview: "Who do you look to when you have specific problems that require a deeper level of expertise than you have? Or who might you see bringing into our relationship beyond your direct team that can advance our success?"

Tony's mantra is, "Give value and do more than expected." The way he does that is to look at every possible way he can give a client more than they even think they want. That may take the form of having the client send his or her executive assistant to his studio to learn how Tony's team operates so efficiently. Over his decades of coaching, he has developed a system of 50 things an executive assistant can do to make an executive 30 percent more productive. Or it may be his outstanding resource arsenal that he shares with his clients, or his best-practice rooms. One of the most impactful ways he gives that extra value to his clients, though, is by sharing his Rolodex or connections.

Each one of your advisors has his or her own set of connections; and if you're smart, you'll tap into that. In fact, if you are paying a coach or any other paid advisor who doesn't share all of his or her resources, you may not be getting full value. Master level advisors will bring their connections to the table to help you get the results you want. For example, when you're meeting with your CPA, the direction of the meeting may suddenly turn to estate planning. A Master level CPA will say, "You know, I know a lot about taxes; but there may be some estate planning distinctions you need here that are beyond my scope of expertise." So the CPA may assemble a team of people – people who have already worked together in the past – working with their different specialties to shortcut your getting the results you want. Or you may be working with your attorney and you get over into the area of trusts. Your attorney may say, "I know about trusts, but I'm not a trust attorney. Let me call in the trust attorney I've teamed up with for 20 years." When he does that, there's a trust transference that goes on; your advisor has just tapped you into his connection that he trusts and has longevity with, and all of a sudden you have the right person to help you solve your problem.

Tony has even said to a few clients who have come to him for coaching, "You know, you don't need my level of expertise. I'm overkill for the particular need you've just explained. I can recommend this person or this person from my Rolodex. Their fees are lower than mine." The clients are astonished, of course, but they're grateful for his honesty and his willingness to share his Rolodex connections with them. You want to have advisors who are very diligent about building relationships that they're willing to bring to the table for your benefit.

Not too long ago, Jay wanted to help the widow of a former partner, who had a legal issue. He sent the issue to David Hammer, his Master level attorney and CPA. David could have made a lot of money by taking on the issue, and the widow certainly had the means to pay. But David went to Jay and said, "I'm not the best person to handle this issue. I have a great relationship with a law firm in Dallas. This law firm has some clout, so when they go to straighten the issue out with the Trust Department of the bank, this law firm will have more influence than I would." Jay was able to help his friend because his advisor was willing to share his Rolodex connection with him and send him to the firm that could help her the most.

When Tony and Jay first got acquainted, Jay had recently been featured in the *Dallas CEO Magazine* (a member of the *D Magazine* family), and he realized that the publisher of the magazine would be an excellent contact for Tony. He made several unsuccessful attempts with phone calls to try to make the connection happen, and he was determined to bypass any roadblocks. He called Tony one day and said, "Bring your driver over." When they arrived, Jay got into the vehicle with them and took Tony to a *D Magazine* event he knew the publisher would be attending. They walked into the event and started shaking hands; and within six minutes Jay was introducing Tony to the publisher, making the connection happen. Then they got back into Tony's vehicle and left. That connection evolved into a valuable relationship with the owner of the magazine, and Tony ended up advising them – all because Jay, as his mentor, was willing and determined to use his connections to make it happen.

You may remember that within two weeks after Jay and Tony first met, Tony bought two first-class round-trip tickets to New York, and they flew up to have lunch with a contact from Jay's Rolodex. That proved to be an invaluable connection for Tony, as well. Not long afterwards, Jay started Biz Owners Ed, and he was able to book speakers for their program from Tony's Rolodex. One was Ron Sturgeon, who was one of Tony's clients. Ron had written an exceptional book called *Getting to Yes with Your Banker*. Tony read the book, loved it, and had his team summarize it. He showed the recap to Jay, who said, "This guy would be a great added value for our mentees." They worked it out, and Ron has turned out to be an excellent speaker for the annual Biz Owners Ed ten-week course. Another was Greg Morse, a banker and entrepreneur, who has also been a great presenter for the organization.

Sharing Rolodex connections has been a natural extension of the exceptional reciprocal relationship that Tony and Jay enjoy as mentor/mentee and coach/client. Time and time again they've used each other's connections to meet various needs, even those not connected to business. For example, Jake, who is a remarkable craftsman who can do just about anything you may need, including carpentry, plumbing, and electric, had worked for Jay for about 30 years and had done all of the beautiful finish work in Jay's office. When Tony needed a quality craftsman to build a Results Lounge in the back of his studio, Jay connected him to Jake. Now Tony has a first-class Results Lounge where his clients can take relaxing breaks.

When you are surrounded with people who are well connected and who are willing to share their Rolodex, the network of connections available to you is like a spider web going out everywhere. Not only do you have connections; but your mentors, coaches, other paid professional advisors, and trusted colleagues have connections, and all of their connections have connections. You can even benefit from the networks of the authors of the books you read by going to their websites and taking advantage of the resources listed there, or by emailing the authors.

Tony grew up benefiting from the connections his parents transferred to him. When he was 14 years old, his dad introduced Tony to the president of the bank and said, "My son needs to establish credit, and he wants to buy a car." His dad cosigned the note; but the point is, this was his way of transferring his relationship with the bank president to Tony.

His dad kept stacks of business cards with rubber bands around them. When someone he knew needed something, he would go through those stacks of business cards, pick the right card out, and make a phone call to someone to make things happen. As a young man, Tony was fascinated with his dad's ability to do that. He thought, "This guy can just call anybody and make anything happen!" So he grew up with the idea that relationships were really good things to have and nourish. Then in 1991 Tony walked into his Los Colinas office and found his business partner instructing his assistant on how to enter the data from his business cards into the computer. It was his first introduction to an electronic database; and from that time on, he determined to have a massive Rolodex that was second to none so he could help his clients, his family, and everyone he advised to be more successful.

Both Jay and Tony agree that if they could give young people starting out in the world today just one piece of advice, it would be to foster and record relationships, keeping detailed records on all the people they meet. With the technology available today, they can enter all of their contacts into a database, classify them, and even sub-classify them – by geography, by specialty, by mutual friends, etc.

Tony was having a meeting in his studio one day, and he had brought in an additional advisor. The advisor was talking to his client, and she made this comment: "When the young people of today bring their resume to the table, they also bring their databases. Their prospective employers want to know how many connections they have in Linkedin, how many they have in Facebook, and how many followers they have on Twitter. And that is part of their value proposition." Tony had never really thought about it before, but he realized what a powerful truth that is – that a Rolodex is a huge asset to bring to the table when applying for a position or for some type of contract.

> "WE MAKE A LIVING BY WHAT WE GET, BUT WE MAKE A LIFE BY WHAT WE GIVE."
> – WINSTON CHURCHILL

When Tony is doing a workshop, he often asks "How many of you, when you get business cards, leave them lying around on your dresser, in your car, or on your desk; and you don't really have a good system for cataloging them?" Usually, most of the people raise their hands very slowly; Then Tony says, "Now, what if I told you that connections are gold? When you meet someone and get a business card, you need to have the discipline to put that into your system so that you capture those relationships." You want advisors who are disciplined enough to do that, so you will have the benefit of all those contacts. Tony has over 30,000 contacts in his Rolodex, and he believes that you can have just a list or you can have a Rolodex. A Rolodex is a list of contacts whom you nourish; you pour in to them, connect with them, and bring value to them. Yes, you should definitely find advisors who have a Rolodex they are willing to share; but you should also have your own Rolodex. Really, all of the contacts you gather are "sub-advisors," if you will – all with the potential to give you advice on their particular areas of expertise or knowledge. They may not be paid advisors, but they can certainly become trusted colleagues after you meet them.

When you have advisors who add their connections to yours, you have the best of both worlds. Even with all of his connections, Tony may sometimes get stumped. He recently called Jay and said, "Do you know anyone who can take out some of the iron on my fence? And do you have a use for some of the iron?" Jay said, "Yes, I know a guy who may be able to help." He called one of his connections (a Biz Owners Ed mentor), who said, "Yeah, I know someone who can do that. Why don't I swap a favor for you?" As it ended up, there were four parties involved, all who were swapping favors for each other. They got the iron removed from Tony's fence and delivered to Jay with no money exchanged; everyone involved just appreciated the fact that they could help their friends out. If you build a life with relationships like that, a lot of great things can happen.

Tony has written over 40 books; and because of the great reciprocal relationship they have, Jay warehouses some of his books for him. Not too long ago, they needed a fork lift to use for about two days to move some of Tony's books around. They looked into renting one, but that would have cost about $1,000. Jay went to his contact list and found a friend who had a forklift. The friend often helped Jay with construction projects, and Jay helped him with business advice. Neither of them ever kept score or sent the other a bill. Because of their long positive relationship, Jerry was happy to loan the forklift and even offered to deliver and pick it up. Because of all the plusses Jay had built up in that relationship, it ended up costing them just a little over $100, instead of the $1,000 it would have cost to rent one. That's a very minor example of the power of connections, but it shows what kinds of things you can expect if you're working with an advisor who really cares about helping you, even beyond the scope of your advisor/advisee relationship.

Because they both love to help people win, Jay and Tony enjoy doing what they call favors in advance. These are favors you do for people without regard to a desired outcome – not necessarily to get something in return. Amazingly, though, people almost always want to give back in some way. Their natural response is to want to return the favor. Since you never know when you might need that favor returned, it's a great idea to store up as many favors in advance as you can. If you make doing favors for others a lifestyle, you'll have a whole bank account of favors to draw from.

For example, when someone calls Tony and says, "Can you help me with this?" he will generally say, "Yes!" When they say, "You didn't even wait to hear what I was going to ask," he says, "Well, if it's reasonable, I'll see if I can help you. That's the way I think. If I can help you out, I'll do it." Sometimes favors in advance involve an expense of energy, or maybe even an expense of money, but it's a mentality you want to embrace. People like to do business with people who do things for them and who work to build a platform of trust. Why not be a giver?

Tony and Zig Ziglar met in 1995 and did several projects together over the years, including making a video series called "Inspire Any Audience." Zig also wrote the foreword to Tony's book by the same name. Zig knew that Tony moved fast, promised fast results, and professed to do favors in advance. About five years ago, Tony got a call from Zig. He said, "Tony, I'd like to meet you for lunch and have a private conversation with you. Would you mind coming over to my club house for lunch?" Tony agreed to meet him; and when they sat down for lunch, Zig started tearing up. He said, "Tony, it's been on my heart for quite a while that I need to apologize to you." He said, "I met you in 1995; and for a long time, I thought because you moved so fast that you were a taker. I had you pegged in my mind as a taker, and I was wrong. Everything you said you'd do, you did; and you're not a taker, you're a giver. I was wrong and I want to apologize to you." And he sat and cried. It amazed Tony that a celebrity with that level of fame would be so humble and take the time to meet with him to get something like that off his mind. To Tony it said, "You know, relationships really do matter." That meant a lot to Tony.

You may remember the story in Chapter 3 about a young lady that Jay mentored; she had been recommended by a psychiatrist, who was Jay's friend and business partner. When she came to Jay for mentoring, Jay gave her Master level advice. Part of that advice was to connect with Culture Index so she could hire the right people. He also immediately connected her with several other people who jumped right in to help her with pressing problems. Those connections from Jay's Rolodex had the impact of a force multiplier that helped to turn her business completely around. He was the right advisor with the right connections to bring into her world.

The impact of the force multiplier can range from the very mundane, as in the example with the fork lift; to a quarter-million-dollar phone call, as was the case with Mitsubishi; to a profitable long-term relationship, as when Jay introduced Tony to the publisher of *D Magazine*. Look for advisors who are willing to share their connections and thus give you the maximum impact. Remember the old proverb, "Two heads are better than one." Whoever wrote that proverb understood the concept of the force multiplier!

V.I.P.s

- As you're doing your due diligence research and the initial interview with potential advisors, find out how well connected they are and how open-minded they are to bringing their team to you.

- One of the most impactful ways advisors can bring value to their advisees is by sharing their Rolodex and connections. If you are paying a coach or any other paid advisor who doesn't share all of his or her resources, you're not getting full value. Master level advisors will bring their connections to the table to help you get the results you want.

- When you are surrounded with people who are well connected and who are willing to share their Rolodex, the network of connections available to you is like a spider web going out everywhere. Not only do you have connections; but your mentors, coaches, other paid professional advisors, and trusted colleagues have connections, and all of their connections have connections.

- A Rolodex is a huge asset to bring to the table when applying for a position or for some type of contract.

- Find advisors who have a Rolodex they are willing to share; but develop your own Rolodex, as well. All of the contacts you gather become "sub-advisors," with the potential to give you advice on their particular areas of expertise or knowledge.

- If you make doing favors for people in your Rolodex a lifestyle, you'll have a whole bank account of favors to draw from.

CONCLUSION

WHAT A DIFFERENCE EXPERIENCE AND KNOWLEDGE CAN MAKE

"To accept good advice is but to increase one's own ability."
—JOHANN WOLFGANG VON GOETHE

Advice matters.

When you picked up this book, you may have agreed with that statement. Hopefully, though, when you put the book down and go back to your life and career, you will be convinced that you must take a more strategic approach to seeking advice.

As co-authors of *Advice Matters*, our purpose for writing the book was to give back to people who want to be smarter – in your decision making, in your business, in your career, in every area of your life. If you didn't believe that advice matters, you probably wouldn't have taken the time to read the book. We hope we have given you insights that lead you to say, "I can be more intentional with the information you've given me. I need to be wise and learn even more from the successes and mistakes of others. I need new thinking to stimulate my reasoning and creative processes and to help me think better. I need to be more strategic in finding the right advisors, meeting with them regularly to seek wisdom and insight, and taking full advantage of the tools they offer me." If that's your takeaway from the book, it's a homerun for all of us.

One last reminder: As you're choosing your advisors, remember that there are five very important criteria to look for:

1. Do they have the track record and experience to lead you where you want to go?

2. Do they have the personal success and expertise to qualify their advice?

3. Do they have an extensive arsenal of tools?

4. How many connections do they have (Rolodex), and are they willing to share their connections with you?

5. Do their values match yours?

Consider what this world would be like if more people were open-minded, recognized the value of strong counsel, and understood that advice matters. How many would experience more wins than losses? How many more great companies would emerge? What great inventions would change the world instead of languishing in someone's basement? How would your life change?

Experience is often the best teacher. The wise person strategically listens to those who are willing to share their experiences, expertise, and recommendations to help him or her win. The benefit of gaining wisdom and knowledge from someone else's years of experience can make an amazing difference in your journey toward Mastery, both personally and professionally.

> "ADVICE IS ONE THING THAT IS FREELY GIVEN AWAY, BUT WATCH THAT YOU ONLY TAKE WHAT IS WORTH HAVING."
> —GEORGE S. CLASON, *THE RICHEST MAN IN BABYLON*

We want to leave you with a story that we believe is the perfect conclusion for this book. Hopefully it will be a reminder that we all benefit greatly from advice. Perhaps more importantly, it will remind us that we often fail to take the time to express our appreciation for advice that shapes our careers and our lives.

When Jay transferred from Eastman Kodak's headquarters in Rochester, New York, to the company's ten-state Southwest Regional Headquarters in Dallas, Texas, in 1964, he met a man named George Kaelber. They worked closely together and quickly became friends. Within less than two years, Jay had become one of George's trusted colleagues. Up to that point, George's highest risk investment had been bank CDs. As a trusted colleague, Jay was able to give solid financial advice to George and guide him into investing in over a dozen higher risk entrepreneurial investments. Over the next 40-plus years, these investments added a few million dollars to the Kaelbers' net worth.

The Kaelbers retired and moved to Arizona several years ago, and George has since passed away. Although Jay and George's widow Jean don't stay in as close touch anymore, Jean was aware that Jay had started the Biz Owners Ed program. As Tony and Jay were doing final editing on this book, Cari, Jay's personal assistant, opened the mail one morning and found a note from Jean, basically thanking Jay for his strong advice. The note read: *"Jay, nice to 'invest' a bit without needing a personal return. Your ideas of the past took care of that. George and I were glad that we were aboard! Jean"* Attached to the note was a check for her $50,000 donation to Biz Owners Ed.

> "WHERE NO COUNSEL IS, THE PEOPLE FALL: BUT IN THE MULTITUDE OF COUNSELLORS THERE IS SAFETY."
> —PROVERBS 11:14, KJV

Advice is Available.

Advice is Valuable.

Advice Does Matter

THE BIZ OWNERS ED STORY

Biz Owners Ed (Biz) was created because a small group of highly successful entrepreneurs believed in small business and the benefits it provides to America's economy and society. This group knew there were numerous entrepreneurs out there who shared their belief and who were willing and eager to give back to, help perpetuate, and help expand this country's seriously committed entrepreneurs by sharing advice from lessons they had learned.

The idea for Biz Owners Ed was originally conceived by Jay Rodgers. Jay is a successful entrepreneur who has bought, grown, and sold over a dozen companies, netting millions of dollars in the process. One of his startups recently sold for over $300 million. Because he appreciates the impact entrepreneurs can have on this great country, he has spent a great deal of his time over the years mentoring them one-on-one. He wanted to have a more powerful impact and a greater influence on more people than he could have with his own limited time, expertise, and contacts. So he stepped back and asked, "What can I devote the rest of my life to that would give ongoing perpetual motion to the fostering and support of successful entrepreneurship?" By leveraging his own Rolodex and connections, he founded Biz Owners Ed.

Jay enlisted the support of his wife Bettye, David Hammer, and Jim Attrell as co-founders. They all shared a concern about the tremendous growth in governmental control of business, which was moving America away from the system that has made it the best country in the world. Although Jay has invested the majority of his time the last 30-plus years helping entrepreneurs, he found he was spending too much time with people who weren't committed or serious enough about building the major companies that are needed in America.

The founders recognized an enormous need for support for serious learners, devoted entrepreneurs, and disciplined high achievers by providing opportunities for them to learn from expert advisors who have successfully dealt with the same challenges they are facing. Higher education was not the answer. Although the higher education system and its tenured professors are well qualified to teach science, literature, history, and many other subjects, most of the professors have never agonized over how they were going to make the next payroll or fund the company's advance. And most have probably never mortgaged their home and future to keep their company alive. Therefore, they're neither equipped nor able to provide the gamut of support required for teaching entrepreneurship. Although Jay taught a Starting Your Own Business class at the University of North Texas and was a guest speaker at the Caruth Institute for Entrepreneurship at SMU's Cox School of Business, he felt he could make a bigger impact in a different setting with a different audience.

Designing and developing the program took over a year and a half, and the first class assembled on January 8, 2013. Tony Jeary, Jay's close personal friend, mentee, and a Master coach, volunteered his expertise, his time, and his energy during the formation of the program, helping with its design. Tony also serves as the key opening speaker for the program, launching the ten-week program each year with a presentation on his Strategic Acceleration methodology of clarity, focus, and execution.

The class is limited to twelve members each year so the participants can interact with the presenters. Also, applicants who don't make a seat in the class each year are invited to audit the program from the gallery, although they are not allowed to interact with the presenters during the program. The guiding principles for selecting class members are: 1) their business brings in over $1 million a year in revenue, 2) they have been in business fewer than seven years, and 3) they have a major ownership in their company. There is one more guideline, and it is the only one cast in concrete: The selection committee must be totally convinced of the individual's commitment and dedication to growing his or her company and creating a multiple of the company's current number of employees. Currently, there is no charge for the selected class members to attend all ten class sessions. However, they must pay a (conditionally) refundable deposit of $1,500 when accepted. The conditions for a full refund are: 1) they must not miss any sessions (they are charged $500 for each session they miss, and 2) they must not be late to any session (they will be charged $100 for each time they are late).

Biz Owners Ed has a full slate of exceptional advisors who are willing and eager to give back and help new entrepreneurs. The organization's criteria for inviting mentors to participate in the program are: 1) that they have built from humble beginnings at least one multi-million-dollar company (some have built two, three, and more), 2) that they commit to give of their time and knowledge, and 3) that they will make at least one or two presentations during the ten-week program. Additionally, as an indication of their sincere desire to help entrepreneurs, they must write a $5,000 check to the Business Owners Ed 501(3)(c) non-profit organization when accepted as a mentor. It is significant that 80 percent of the individuals invited by Biz to become a mentor have accepted the invitation. Many go beyond the ten-week formal program and have established on-going mentor/mentee relationships with its graduates.

The Biz Owners Ed founders are very deliberate and cautious about inviting guest speakers, most of whom own businesses that service and support small businesses. Guest speakers are there to provide only immediate and actionable information of value to entrepreneurs, not to solicit in any form or fashion clients for their particular businesses. Any guest speaker uttering a single solicitous line during the presentation is not invited back.

Biz Owners Ed has been tremendously successful, and the stories of the growth and successes of its class members are numerous and wonderful to celebrate. A member of its first class in January 2013 owned a business that had gross revenue of $10.5 million in 2012. He credits the Biz Owners Ed program with playing a significant role in moving his company revenues to over $24 million in 2014.

The non-profit organization has turned out to be a win for everyone – certainly for Jay, personally, and for the other founders; but it's also a tremendous win for the mentees, the mentors, the presenters, and the observers in the gallery. Everyone is winning, including the great country of America!

Since every Biz Owners Ed graduate has been ecstatic about the program and appreciative of what he or she has learned, Biz is happy to provide a contact list of all 37 graduates since the program's inception.

Although the program currently serves only the DFW market, the Biz Owners Ed founders stand ready to consider the request of anyone desiring to establish a sister program in their market, and to provide a great deal of support if the request is approved.

APPENDICES

GLOSSARY: TOP TONY JEARY COINED PHRASES

- **Clarity, Focus, Execution**: The three core principles for Tony Jeary's *Strategic Acceleration* methodology.

- **High Leverage Activities (HLAs)**: The base methodology of Tony Jeary's bestselling book *Strategic Acceleration*; HLAs are efficient actions that result in the most valuable outcomes.

- **Life Team**: A group of hand-picked individuals who help you make decisions and execute. Examples could include your spouse, executive assistant, coach, mentors, colleagues, readers, driver, lawyer, trainer, CPA, etc.

- **MOLO (More Of, Less Of)**: A simple exercise to help an individual or organization identify what they need to eliminate so they can focus on what matters most. An evaluation of what should be done More Often and Less Often will ensure time is best invested on proactive, productive High Leverage Activities (HLAs) instead of on time-wasting, less effective tasks. Top leaders model self-reflection and continuous improvement.

- **Operational Mastery**: Performing at the top level, better than great, often leading to extended value of an organization of any size.

- **Production Before Perfection (PBP)**: The principle that we must not allow the fear of potential missteps to prevent us from taking effective action now.

- **Strategic Acceleration**: Tony Jeary's proven methodology that helps people get clear, stay focused, and efficiently execute relevant, High-Value activities, thereby delivering results and success faster.

- **Strategic Clarity**: Being intentional about your understanding as well as ensuring understanding at all levels in an organization

ABOUT THE AUTHORS

Tony Jeary is a results strategist. Many call him The RESULTS Guy™ because of this simple fact—he helps clients get the right results faster. He is a unique and powerful facilitator and subject matter expert who has advised over 1,000 clients and published over forty books. His studio process of live note taking, combined with his *Strategic Acceleration* methodology, is a secret weapon for his special clients. Tony has invested the past 25+ years developing facilitation processes and systems that allow him and his team to accelerate results, doing planning meetings in a single day, and producing results that often take days, weeks, and months in a single eight-hour session. That's a rare gift.

The world's greatest CEOs recognize the importance of thinking, strategy, and communication; and many seek Tony for all three of these. He's a gifted encourager who helps clarify visions.

The primary goal of all leaders is to enhance value and communicate their vision effectively so that their teams can execute that vision in the marketplace. Tony personally coaches presidents and CEOs of Walmart, TGI Friday's, New York Life, Firestone, Samsung, Ford, Texaco, and SAM's; even those on the Forbes richest 400 engage Tony for his advice. Tony personally helps these top leaders: define their goals; accelerate their opportunities; create, establish, and build their personal brands and careers; deliver powerful paradigm-shifting presentations; grow their leadership abilities; and accelerate the right results faster! He and/or his whole firm can be booked through his business manager. Tony Jeary International can be retained to do amazing things to support accelerated RESULTS.

Jay D. Rodgers has been and continues to be active in the formation of entrepreneurial enterprises. His involvement includes vision, funding, strategic planning, and exit dealings. He is dedicated to helping committed entrepreneurs and has founded Biz Owners Ed, a non-profit devoted to mentoring entrepreneurs.

Jay has personally founded, grown, and sold over a dozen businesses, including: Smart Start Inc., now the nation's largest breath-alcohol ignition interlock company with over 1,300 service locations in the U.S. and in 6 foreign countries; Physician Staffing Resources, Inc. (PSR), a national emergency medicine physician management company serving over 2,000 ER doctors; Healthcare Staff Resources, Inc. (HSR), which provides healthcare professionals to healthcare facilities nationwide; Ranchland, Inc., a corporate outing and convention ranch destination; Tri-C Business Forms; and Family Staffing Solutions. His most recent start-up is Rhino Fleet Tracking, a GPS monitoring and tracking company. In 1993, he completed the three-year Owners & Presidents Management (OPM) Program at Harvard. Jay served as a guest lecturer at SMU's Caruth Institute of Entrepreneurs. Jay is currently working on a book filled with stories that provide valuable lessons he learned from his entrepreneurial life.

WHAT CAN TONY JEARY INTERNATIONAL DO FOR YOU?

CULTURE CHANGE

We change company cultures. *Strategic Acceleration* is a methodology that gets the right results faster for selected clients that have a true appetite for advancing their vision to reality quicker. Our *Strategic Acceleration* methodology is foolproof because it's not theory, academia, or new. It's proven, based on real results, and works every time. Please Watch the 90-second video on "Change Your Thinking, Change Your Results" at changeyourthinkingchangeyourresults.com. We get results!

STRATEGIC PLANNING

Let us work with you to develop a customized strategic plan for more clarity, focus, and execution, hence more accelerated results! We develop powerful plans in a single day that take most people three days minimum and often weeks. We have a custom-built Strategic Acceleration Studio designed specifically for this offering.

RESULTS COACHING

Having coached many of the world's top CEOs and earners, Tony understands the need for speed in today's marketplace. Benefit from 20 years of best practices from the best of the best. If you operate an organization that has millions to be made, and you're interested in sharpening your executive leadership effectiveness, let's talk.

CULTURE-CHANGING WEB TRAININGS

Most organizations struggle with weekly meetings and poor email standards, resulting in too many meetings and too many emails, costing valuable time. Results are dramatically being hurt because of people operating in overwhelm. Tony has taken his expertise and developed simple 45-minute web trainings that can save thousands of non-productive hours for an organization and greatly impact results. Let us discuss impacting your culture. Subjects include (among others):

Email Effectiveness

Engagement

The Art of Results

Influence

Meeting Mastery

Change Your Thinking

Time Effectiveness

KEYNOTE SPEECHES

Tony is available for unique keynote experiences that dramatically impact audiences of all sizes. Topics include *Strategic Acceleration* and Leverage, among others.

OTHER BOOKS BY TONY

Change Your Thinking, Change Your Results	changethinkingchangeresults.com
Strategic Acceleration	strategicacceleration.com
Business Ground Rules	businessgroundrules.com
Ultimate Health	ultimatehealth-book.com
Life Is a Series of Presentations	mrpresentation.com
How to Gain 100 Extra Minutes a Day	tonyjeary.com
Designing Your Own Life	tonyjeary.com

To discuss how we can bring value to you and your organization, email us at info@tonyjeary.com or call us at 817.430.9422.

Notes

NOTES

NOTES

NOTES

NOTES

NOTES

NOTES

NOTES

NOTES

NOTES

NOTES

NOTES

NOTES

CPSIA information can be obtained at www.ICGtesting.com
Printed in the USA
BVOW06s1212110816

458580BV00040B/198/P